A MAN'S GAME:

THE BIRTH OF MANCUNIAN FOOTBALL & THE ORIGINS OF MANCHESTER CITY FC

A MAN'S GAME

Andrew Keenan

BOOKS & DOXEY

First published in May 2013 by Books & Doxey Press

This edition published November 2013

Copyright © Andrew Keenan 2013

ISBN-13: 978-1466311497

Cover design by Tony Keenan

To Michelle

CONTENTS

ACKNOWLEDGEMENTS

All history writers owe a debt of gratitude to those who came before them. From Bob Roden and Fred Johnson – who wrote the first detailed history of City in 1930 – to David Williams, Bill Miles, Dennis Chapman, Andrew Waldon, Ray Goble, John Maddocks and Steve Kay. Tony Heap, who in the 1970s first delved into the social history surrounding the club's formative years, deserves a mention alongside published authors Andrew Ward, Keith Mellor, Ian Penney and Gary James. Thanks must also go to Paul Toovey, whose exhaustive research resulted in many important discoveries about the club's early years.

I'd like to especially thank Neil Ogden, whose research on Manchester's cricket history has yielded great finds in the football field (particularly regarding he location of early grounds), and also Jack Greenald, a dedicated archivist of Manchester's Orange Order. The incredibly friendly and professional staff at Ashton library also deserve a special mention, and I'd also like to acknowledge the creators of Open Street Map for allowing free use of their maps.

But most of all I want to thank my partner Michelle, a specialist in evangelical history, for her rigorous critique of my research and her cold, calculating use of red font.

CHAPTER 1

FOOTBALL COMES TO MANCHESTER

No-one will ever know when football was first played in Manchester. It may have been introduced by Roman soldiers, who built the Mamucium fort in AD79 in Castlefield and probably brought with them a rugby-like game called "Harpastum". The game's origins may go back further, to pagan times, when a Celtic tribe called the Brigante claimed the area as their territory. Or perhaps it goes back further still, to when someone first kicked an inflated animal bladder around some time after the last ice age ended roughly 11,700 years ago.

The first record of "a game of ball" being played in Britain was in the 9th century. Around the 1170s William FitzStephen's *A Description of London* provided the first detailed account of the game, which was played on a public holiday called "Carnival". After spending the morning watching cock-fighting with their teachers "all the youths of the city goes out into the fields for the very popular game of ball." FitzStephen continues,

> "The scholars of each school have their own ball,
> and almost all the workers of each trade have theirs
> also in their hands. The elders, the fathers, and the
> men of wealth come on horseback to view the
> contests of their juniors, and in their fashion sport
> with the young men; and there seems to be aroused
> in these elders a stirring of natural heat by viewing
> so much activity and by participation in the joys of
> unrestrained youth."

An Edwardian depiction of a 14th century football match

For the next few hundred years the game served largely as an outlet for local rivalries and was played on public holidays. According to James Walvin's *The People's Game*, medieval football was an "ill-defined contest between indeterminate crowds of youth, often played in riotous fashion". Reports of violence and damage to property during matches were numerous, injuries were common and deaths not unheard of. The game's effects were particularly felt in cities. In 1608 the local authorities in Manchester complained that

"There has been heretofore great disorder in our towne of Manchester, and the inhabitants thereof greatly wronged and charged with makinge and amendinge of their glasse windows broken yearelye and spoyled by a companye of lewd and disordered persons using that unlawfull exercise of playinge with the ffote-ball in ye streets".

The Manchester Leet court imposed a hefty fine of 1s 2d for anyone caught playing football, and appointed six officers to enforce the ban. The violence associated with football resulted in more than 30 royal and local prohibitions across the country between 1324 and 1667. Puritans, unhappy the sport was being played on Sundays, also hindered its growth. But it was probably the 18th-century enclosures – which saw vast areas of common land transferred into private ownership – that most hindered the game, particularly as in rural matches the goals could be three miles or more apart.

One place it was free to flourish was the public school. The first reference to public school football was at Eton in 1519 where a game was played "with a ball full of wynde". According to Walvin, early public school football "closely resembled the popular folk game" though in a smaller playing area and with fewer participants. The game spread to other public schools in the early 19th century at a time when they were plagued by violent disorder (a riot at Rugby school in 1797 was put down by the army and one of Winchester school's many riots was quelled by the militia). But in the 1830s and 1840s the idea of "Muscular" Christianity – which linked physical fitness to spirituality and good morals – took hold in public schools. And under the watchful gaze of educationalists the rules of the game began to be codified.

After the first set of rules were created at Eton in 1815, other public schools devised their own codes. This caused confusion when the schoolboys reached university so in 1848 Cambridge University drew up its set of rules, which appear to be based on the Eton game. But this did not solve the problem of competing codes. The Sheffield Rules, created in 1858, became popular in the north, and in 1862 were joined by two new sets of rules: a revised version of Rugby Rules, which became the basis of rugby football, and Uppingham Rules, created by the co-author of the 1848 Cambridge rules, E J Thring. Even individual clubs had their own set of rules. For instance, in 1863 the Lincoln Football Club was playing a code that was "drawn from" Marlborough, Eton and Rugby rules.

So in October 1863 representatives of Eton, Westminster, Harrow, Winchester and Rugby schools announced they were to form a club – called the "Miserable Shinners" – "in order to arrange one general set of rules for football". They failed in their task, but succeeded in creating the first Football Association rules, which were adopted by the newly-formed FA in London on 26 October 1863.

Commonly known as London association rules, they were also based on the Eton game, which was played with a "small and light" ball. They allowed for an unlimited number of players per side and no maximum height was specified for the goals. Players were awarded a free-kick for a "fair catch" (where a player makes a mark with his heel), throw-ins were similar to rugby line-outs, and attacking teams were awarded a free-kick 15 yards from the goal line for a rugby-style "try". The rules also stated that no player could be between any opponent and the goal when the ball was played to him, limiting forward passes to high punts up the field.

However, Rule 10, which stated that "neither tripping nor hacking shall be allowed, and no player shall use his hands to hold or push his adversary", represented a fundamental break with other codes – and became the basis of the modern game of football.

The Rugby City

But it was the rugby code that established itself in Manchester. The first known side were called Manchester Football Club, and were formed following a trial game at Oakwood Park in Pendlebury in 1860. They initially played near Alexandra Park in Moss Side and probably wore scarlet and black hoops. The club's captain was Richard Sykes, a former football captain of Rugby School and a member of Stockport's wealthiest family. His grandfather, William, had introduced cotton bleaching to Edgeley in 1792, and the 21-year-old Richard would later prove he was cut from similar cloth. In the 1880s he bought 45,000 acres of farmland in North Dakota and founded five towns there, naming one after his birthplace of Edgeley. Aged 65, he married a 25-year-old Manchester woman, moved to a spa resort in California and fathered two sons with her.

For its first few years rugby football was the preserve of gentlemen such as Sykes. However, in September 1864 Manchester's mayor, John Marsland Bennett, revealed a new sporting vision in a speech at the first Manchester Athletic Festival at Old Trafford. He declared that

> "At our great public schools boys are compelled
> (willingly or unwillingly) to take part in cricket,
> football, and other manly exercises. Why then,
> should not that vigour which the upper classes gain
> by manly sports at our public schools and
> universities, be shared in by young men in our
> warehouses and manufactories?"

It was the first reference to football being a desirable sport for Manchester working men, and the message was timely. The codification of football rules coincided with the reduction of the working week, from six days to five plus a half-day Saturday. The shorter working week was introduced after research carried out in the mid-19th century revealed that reducing working hours usually resulted in a net gain in productivity. It also meant that the punishingly-long working hours endured by millions of people over the previous decades had been of no benefit to anyone.

This extra leisure time led to the spread of unregulated – and often drunken – Saturday football, despite the fact that playing the game was punishable by a fine of five shillings or more. At a shareholders' meeting of Trafford's Manchester Botanical Gardens in April 1862 one speaker referred to the problem of Saturday afternoon football, while another speaker (called Mr Petty) claimed that "annoyance had been caused to ladies and others by the playing of football".

A solution was found in the dozen or so gymnastics clubs that had sprung up in Manchester since the 1830s. Most had been built by the city's literary societies as a means of combating disease, and initially they focused on sports such as running, throwing and boxing. One of the largest gymnasiums was run by the Manchester Athenaeum, a society created for "advancement and diffusion of knowledge", whose headquarters on Princess Street is now the home of the Manchester Art Gallery. On 13 October 1866 it was the setting for a meeting of Manchester's Union of Working Men's Clubs, which represented the area's Mechanics Institutes. These Institutes had been created as sister organisations of the literary clubs, with the aim of drawing the working classes "from scenes of dissipation and vice, by furnishing them with rational employment for their leisure". And it was at this meeting that team sport was proposed as a solution to the "problem" of increased leisure time.

Chairing the meeting, J McKerrow called on the Union to find "the best means of counter-acting the evil agencies of the public-house". Up until this point the Mechanics Institutes had focused on providing educational lectures with titles such as "The history and manufacture of coal gas" and "The general properties of arsenic". Declaring that these "were generally too philosophical and scientific" for the working man, McKerrow stressed the importance of matching "the attractive influence of the public-house". It "was necessary to have a class of institutions to which they would more freely resort, and in which they would have confidence," he said. Another speaker, Rev. Mr Squire from Preston, called for "the arrangement of meetings for social amusements and group discussions; also for chess, cricket, football, gymnastics, and other matches".

Less than two months later, on Saturday 11 December, a club called Hulme Athenaeum – an organisation borne out of a merger between a literary society and a Mechanics Institute – played its first recorded game of rugby football, against Sale. The match appears to mark the beginnings of a new form of recreation: the Saturday afternoon game, played by working men under public school rules.

The rugby game now spread rapidly throughout Manchester and for the next few years appears to have been the only football code played regularly in the city. It's not clear why it prospered at the expense of other codes, though it may be connected to the fact that James Prince Lee, Manchester's bishop between 1848 and 1869, was formerly an assistant master at Rugby School. A pro-rugby bias can also be detected in the Manchester press, which often neglected to cover the association game throughout the 1860s and 1870s.

By November 1874 at least 24 rugby clubs had been established in the Manchester area, while the only association match listed in local newspapers that month was a 13-a-side game between the 8th Cheshire Rifles and Stoke-upon-Trent at Macclesfield. But the association game was beginning to blossom elsewhere in Britain's industrial districts as working hours were reduced. According to Peter Bailey's *Leisure and Class in Victorian England*, by 1870 the half-day Saturday "was realized in most factories, mines, and workshops". Bailey notes that the Education Act passed that year, which ensured that "a school should be placed within the reach of every English child", also led to the spread of organized games. In the early 1870s football took root in Sheffield, Birmingham and the Potteries. But it was the Lancashire mill towns that did the most to promote the game from 1874 onwards.

Manchester's First Association Club

Football had been a popular pastime for Lancashire mill workers since at least the early 1850s. On 22 October 1853 the *Manchester Times*, reporting on a meeting of around 2,000 striking mill workers on Preston Marsh, noted that "several hundreds were engaged, both before and after the meeting, in playing at football". The number of players involved suggests that this was a form of medieval football which, according to Adrian Harvey's *Football: The First Hundred Years*, remained a popular working-class pastime throughout this period. In October 1854 two boys received 14 days hard labour after stealing 11 footballs from a shoemaker's shop in Heywood and selling them on for 2d each (a fifth of their value). And in April 1860 the *National Magazine's* "Sketch of Stockport" carried an account of football being played near the Bow Garrets public house beside an early form of terracing – called "bongs" – on what is now the playing field behind the Lark Hill Nursery School in Edgeley.

> "'Bongs' they are called, and will be, in all probability, as long as they endure for the boys and young men to assemble on in the evenings, for cricket and football. They are simply masses of irregular rocks; or more correctly, one, intersected by cuttings, rude steps, and paths, and covered with course herbage."

But from the late 1850s new clubs, playing variants of the association game, sprang up around the country. They were founded by young wealthy men who had played the game at public schools. By the second half of the 1870s they had sparked the creation of working men's teams, formed under the guidance of the clergy and mill owners. In Lancashire the spark glowed brightest in Blackburn and Darwen, two proud mill towns separated by only a few fields. Intense local rivalry resulted in huge attendances at games (Blackburn's population was around

90,000 and Darwen's 30,000) which, in turn, introduced profit and professionalism to the sport.

From there the game spread down the railways to other mill towns, including the outer-lying parts of what is now Greater Manchester, and in particular, Bolton. It arrived in Manchester towards the end of 1875. On 2 October a letter to the *Athletic News* proposed the formation of Manchester's first association club. It was called Manchester Association and its home ground "was on land adjoining" Pepperhill Farm in Moss Side. The club was made up of gentlemen players who had moved to the area, and managed by Hon. Sec. Stuart G Smith, who had previously played football for Nottinghamshire.

As there were no other association sides in the area, the club's first recorded match, on 13 November 1875, was against themselves. According to the *Guardian,* a team chosen by Smith beat club member J Nall's side by one goal to nil. The match was played at Moss Side, and was the first recorded game of association football played in Manchester. On 29 January Manchester Association were scheduled to play away to Stoke – the city's oldest club who later became known as Stoke City – but there is no record of the match being played. The next reference to the club was on 15 February, when the *Manchester Courier* published a letter (page 10) revealing its formation.

It was under the pen-name "Nyren", suggesting it was written by a cricket enthusiast who probably took his name from John Nyren, author of the most famous cricket book of the Victorian age. The letter's observations on the dangers of rugby were prompted by the violent death of a player. In the early hours of 6 February a 16-year-old music seller's assistant from Moss Side, named Joseph Ison, died from injuries sustained in a rugby match the previous day. His team, Egerton, were playing local rivals Fallowfield Rovers at Chorlton. It was a fixture that had previously resulted in bad blood (in March 1875 Egerton abandoned a home match against Fallowfield following a disputed goal), and Ison's injuries were the result of an illegal "charge" by a Fallowfield player. His death sparked intense debate on the dangers of the rugby code, and also resulted in the Egerton club disbanding. At the inquest two days later coroner

Mr F Price condemned the "brutish" aspect of the game and warned that further cases could result in manslaughter charges.

> There has lately been a club started in Manchester under the rules of the association, which are much less dangerous than those of Rugby, inasmuch as tackling in any form, either by body or legs, scrimmaging or butting, are not allowed. Charging is allowed, but the penalty of charging off side is a free kick, which has a good effect; indeed, charging altogether is discouraged. This is true football, no one being allowed to handle the ball at all except the goal-keeper, who must at once kick or throw it, but cannot run with it. If these rules were adopted more about Manchester we should hear less about the rough game of football, and there would be less chance of accidents; speed and skill would take the place of strength, which last is accounted of small moment in the game. This game is very popular about London, Glasgow, or Sheffield, where it is well understood, and draws large numbers of spectators.
>
> I have no connection with either of the games, but have seen both played, and would recommend these suggestions to the careful consideration of all engaged in them.—Yours, &c.,   NYREN.

Manchester Association's next recorded match was on 11 March 1876, when they lost 1-0 to Broughton Wasps at Lower Broughton. Wasps was a rugby club, and it's possible it was experimenting with what was considered a less violent code. The exact location of the ground is unclear, though it may have been the site where Manchester United's Cliff training ground was later established.

> Broughton Wasps v. Manchester Association.—Played at Broughton (under the association rules), and won by the Wasps by one goal to nil.

The Manchester Courier's report of the 11 March game

Both clubs were made up of gentlemen players, and in December the elite character of the association game in Manchester was illustrated by Manchester Association's line-up for their "Grand Football Match" against Sheffield at Longsight.

Manchester Association team for 16 December 1876:
J F Richardson (goal), A B Potter (Eton), G A Jones, F J Haigh, S G Smith (Notts) (capt), A Mason (Shropshire Wanderers), T A C Hampson (Oxford), J A Railton jr (Forest School), C F Edwards (Shropshire Wanderers, replaced by Starey for match), H Ellis (Forest School), R A Thorp, Mr C Mason (umpire).

The side contained seven men who had formerly played for gentlemen's teams outside Manchester. These young men, from the country's top public schools, had been tutored to become rulers of an empire. Watching them wasn't cheap (for the admission price of one shilling you could spend the day at the nearby Belle Vue pleasure gardens) and neither was the post-match entertainment. The corresponding fixture in 1878 was followed by a dinner party at Sheffield's Imperial Hotel, where players from both clubs drank champagne and sang popular songs, including the bawdy Kafoozlem, the "Harlot of Jerusalem".

Manchester's first association match with Sheffield resulted in a 4-0 defeat. Despite that, on 18 December 1876 the *Sheffield Daily Telegraph* was optimistic about the city's prospects.

> "With fine weather and good matches, there is no
> reason why association football should not in time
> be as popular and well supported in Manchester, as
> it now is in Glasgow and Sheffield. The time may
> or may not be far distant, but eventually the brutal
> rough Rugby rules will give way before the more
> artistic and superior game adopted by the
> association."

But the return match, on 24 February 1877, was a humiliation.

A similar Manchester line-up to the December fixture were beaten 14-0 at Sheffield's Bramall Lane ground. According to *The Graphic* it was a score that "has never been seen" on a football field, "so easily did cotton go down before steel". The *Sheffield Telegraph* later noted that Manchester "had not gone through that thorough system of training necessary to ensure success", though as the match was probably played under Sheffield Rules this might also reflect their unfamiliarity with the code.

However, the separation of the two codes was not to last much longer. On 20 October 1877 Manchester Association played Broughton Wasps for a second time. According to the *Courier,* the match was played under "new association rules", an amalgamation of London, Sheffield and Scottish Association rules that had been agreed six months earlier. The new rules established corner-kicks, throw-ins and offside as universal parts of the game. All three associations had made compromises in order to unify the rules. The London FA, for instance, wanted to keep rugby-style line-outs instead of throw-ins, while the Scots wanted a four-man offside rule. However, by creating a code that could be used throughout England and Scotland, association football was now primed for rapid growth.

The new code had certainly attracted the interest of Broughton Wasps, which had been a solid rugby club up to this point. Indeed, the match report noted the number of free-kicks for handball conceded by Wasps, who were "accustomed to pick up the ball at every opportunity". However, it appears that Wasps did not pursue any further interest in the association game. For the time-being the only "true" football club in the city was Manchester Association.

On 3 November 1877 they became the first Manchester side to take part in the FA Cup, losing 3-1 at home to Darwen in the first round. The game was played at a new home ground in Eccles, described as "not a very good one, being rather small". The change was probably connected to the formation that season of the city's second association club, called Birch. It originated from the Birch rugby club, which was based at the Longsight Cricket Club.

Located to the south-west of Belle Vue Gardens beside the railway line L&NWR, Longsight Cricket Club could now lay claim to being the epicentre of Manchester sport. As well as having links with the Manchester Athenaeum, which helped organise the first Longsight Athletics Festival there in 1869, it had close ties with the nearby Belle Vue pleasure gardens, whose long sporting tradition included the holding of swimming galas and would soon include the creation of a curling team.

Lacrosse 9 Football 1

On 27 June 1876 Longsight Cricket Club hosted the first ever game of lacrosse to be staged in England. It was played between a team of Canadian gentlemen and a team of Iroquois Indians and attracted a crowd of up to 4,000 spectators paying 1 to 2 shillings each. The game sparked the creation of the Manchester Lacrosse Club a week later. By the following March three other lacrosse teams – Broughton, Farnworth and Stockport – had been formed, and by December 1879 had been joined by Cheadle, South Manchester, Blackley, Stretford and Heaton Mersey.

tion. The Canadians are represented by Dr. W. G. Beene (captain), Messrs. Angus Grant, H. Wylie Becket, T. G. Ralston, S. Massey, W. B. Ross, R. Summerhayes, F. C. A. M'Indoe, D. E. Bowie, T. E. Hodgson, H. C. Joseph, J. T. Green, and G. S. Hubbell. The Iroquois are:—Teir Karoraire (Blue Spotted), Aton8a Tekanennao8iheu (Hickory Wood Split), Sha8atis Anasotako (Pick the Feather), Sha8atis Aientonni (Hole in the Sky), Sishe Taiennontii (Flying Name), Aton8a Teronko8a (The Loon), Sishe Ononsanoron (Deer House), Saksarii Tontariiakon (Crossing the River), Tier Skanenrati (Outside the Multitude), Rasar Kanentakeron (Scattered Branches), Kor Kanentakeron (Spruce Branches), Saksarii Shakosennakete (Great Arm), and Alon8a Ton8nnata (Wild Wind).

The line-ups for the lacrosse match on 27 June 1876

13

In the association game, however, the number of clubs in the city was about to halve. Manchester Association had lost all of their six matches in the 1877-78 season, scoring just two goals and conceding 24. That included a 7-0 defeat away to Derby Grammar School in October and a 6-0 loss at Nottingham two months later, and meant that the club's record against teams from outside Manchester stood at P9 L9 F3 A44.

Manchester Association's last two games of the season had been played at the Longsight Cricket Club, where Birch had experienced a "fairly successful" season. Around the end of the 1877-78 season the two clubs merged, renaming themselves Manchester Association Wanderers. The club now played home games at Whalley Range, on land adjoining Manchester FC's ground. Although officially a merger, a better description would be that Birch had incorporated the remnants of Manchester Association. The line-up for the first match of the season, a 4-1 defeat to Stoke in November 1878, contained only one Manchester Association player, former captain Stuart Smith.

On 12 November 1878 Wanderers were one of the first sides to play under floodlights. The match at Stoke may also have been the first to be played with a white ball, introduced in order to be picked up better by the 6,000 candles of light each of the two floodlights produced (roughly 2% of the light produced in a modern-day stadium). The first ever floodlit football match had been played on 14 October, in front of 17,000-30,000 spectators at Bramall Lane cricket ground. On 29 October the first floodlit game had taken place in Manchester, when 8,000-10,000 watched a rugby match between Broughton Wasps and Swinton at Lower Broughton. The Wanderers played two floodlit matches in Stoke, but neither were a success. Snowstorms ensured low turnouts, and weather-damage to the lights caused occasional blackouts. An amused *Staffordshire Sentinel* noted that on several occasions "when a player had to run the ball, and was about to shoot at goal, the light would go dim".

The prospects for Manchester football around this time looked no brighter. Earlier that month only a "small number" of spectators had watched Wanderers lose 4-1 to Stoke at Whalley Range, while just 200 attended the 1-0 home defeat to Sheffield on 22 March. Struggling for funds, on 26 April 1879 they hosted an "association tournament among Rugby clubs" at Whalley Range. The Manchester press neglected to cover it, but the *Sheffield Daily Telegraph* reported that sides from three rugby clubs – Broughton Rangers, Birch FC and Cheetham FC – took part. The report, though, saw little hope for Manchester football.

"There was only a small attendance, and the teams who contested only represented three clubs, whereas the promoters advertised six clubs. The affair was superintended by the Manchester Association Football Club, who after a disastrous season as regards gate money and results of matches are said to be low in funds, and the tournament was asserted to be the last struggle of association enthusiasts. The association game has apparently no fascination in Manchester."

By this time Stoke had become a hotbed of association football, with "more than 20 good clubs" created between 1874-77. Nottinghamshire and Birmingham had a similar number, while Sheffield had approximately twice that. But, with the association game in Manchester facing extinction, on 3 May 1879 Association Wanderers were thrown a financial lifeline when an exhibition match was held at Turton Moor near Bolton. A combined Wanderers, Queen's Park (Glasgow) and Bolton Football Club side played a combined Darwen and Blackburn Rovers team in front of 3,000 spectators. According to the *Derby Daily Telegraph,* proceeds of the gate were "devoted towards wiping off the debts of the Manchester Wanderers and augmenting the funds of the Lancashire Association".

The club survived, though Manchester remained one of football's last unconquered outposts. By the spring of 1879 Lancashire football was getting national attention after Darwen took Eton to two replays in the semi-final of the FA Cup. But in October Association Wanderers attracted "barely 50 spectators" for the 3-1 loss to Sheffield at Brook's Bar, despite the weather being "delightfully fine". That winter 40 teams took part in the first round of the new Lancashire FA Challenge Cup. Dominated by clubs from the mill towns of Blackburn, Darwen and Bolton, the only entrants from Manchester were Association Wanderers,

By 1880 association football had become firmly established as a national game. The *Birmingham Mail*, for instance, revealed that "70 or more legitimate matches" were commonly played each Saturday in the city. But in January that year a letter was published in the *Manchester Chronicle* reminding readers that "there is a method of playing football as football, not as handball". Such was rugby's dominance that in March 1880 entrepreneur James Reilly unveiled plans for a rugby World Cup in Manchester. It was to be staged at his Pomona pleasure gardens in Trafford and prizes included solid gold medals and a cup worth over £200.

PROPOSED INTERNATIONAL FOOTBALL CONTEST IN MANCHESTER.—Mr. James Reilly, the proprietor of Pomona Gardens, proposes next season to offer prizes of the value of 300 guineas for a football contest open to the world. The first prize will consist of a cup worth 200 guineas, to be designed and made to suit the wishes of the winning team, together with solid gold medals, of the total value of 50 guineas, for presentation to the players. The second prize will be a handsome silver cup, or other similar trophy, of the value of 50 guineas. There will be no restriction as to entries, and it is expected that the leading football clubs will take part in the contest. The arrangements will be entrusted to a committee selected from some of the principal associations, and no effort will be spared to invest the event with national significance. The matches will be played in the large grounds attached to Pomona Palace, which, being well drained and laid out, are well adapted for a trial of such importance.

Note that rugby was referred to as football at this time

The only other association club in the region was Hurst, established in Ashton-under-Lyne in 1878 and likely to be connected to the Hurst cotton mill. But on 1 September 1880 a letter to the *Manchester Courier* announced the creation of a new association club in Harpurhey.

ASSOCIATION FOOTBALL.

To the Editor of the Manchester Courier.

Sir,—Coming from the south I am surprised at the almost total absence in Manchester of the association game. Doubtless many of your readers, who are old association men, or who would be football players, but do not care for the rough hand-play and handling of the Rugby game, would be glad to assist in the formation of a club to play the association rules. I have just started such a club in this district, and shall be glad of the co-operation of any of your readers. Your kind insertion of the above will oblige.—Yours, &c.,

OLD ASSOCIATION.

23, Palatine-street, Harpurhey, September 1.

Living at that address were the Glass family, who had moved to the area from London. Norman Glass, 47, was a non-conformist minister (listed as "Independent Minister No Charge" in the census) and probably the author of the letter. Two institutions had been crucial to the spread of football throughout Lancashire: the cotton mills and the church. The Harpurhey club, which became known as Manchester Arcadians, had links to both. The Glass family were active in a local Sunday school, while Norman's sons, 21-year-old Percy and 19-year-old Herbert, both worked in a cotton warehouse. But Harpurhey was also within touching distance of east Manchester's iron industry, by now one of the driving forces of Britain's economy. Its giant foundries and workshops would soon play a key role in the birth of two clubs that would later be known around the globe: Manchester City and Manchester United.

At the start of the rugby season on 9 October 1880, the *Gorton*

Reporter records seven rugby games in the Manchester area and only one association game, Hurst's 4-0 defeat to Blackburn Park Road at Ashton Moss. Over the following three weeks the paper recorded 60 rugby games and only one association match, Hurst v Middleton on 23 October.

But on 13 November a new club, St Mark's, played its first recorded match against Baptist of Macclesfield. They took their name from St Mark's Anglican church in West Gorton, and were the first known association side in the Manchester area to be made up of working men. The club also marked a meeting point between cotton and iron. The church's construction was paid for by owners of local locomotive manufacturer Beyer Peacock, while St Mark's officials also held senior positions at the area's largest employer, Union Iron, which produced machinery for cotton mills.

A week later three new Mancunian football clubs played their first recorded match. Clarence Association, which probably originated from the Clarence cotton mill in Stalybridge, played Broadbottom in front of 200 spectators. Manchester Arcadians also played their first recorded match that day, while another new club with mill connections from north Cheshire, called Bollington, played Hurst. Saturday 20 November also saw the first appearance of another Manchester club. They were the Newton Heath LYR's carriage works team, who later became known as Manchester United.

The date of Newton Heath's creation has, for many years, been a source of uncertainty. The first written account of the club's history, in the 1905-6 *Book of Football*, was especially vague about the club's starting point.

> "Somewhere about 1878 there were Association
> football clubs in a small way in the Manchester
> district, and one of the best known of these was
> undoubtedly Newton Heath."

The discovery of a fixture list for the 1882-83 season, which stated that the Newton Heath (LYR) Cricket and Football Club was formed in 1878, appeared to confirm matters. However, in

1878 "football" in Manchester referred solely to the rugby code, while soccer was referred to as either "association" or "football (association rules)". More significantly, a newly-discovered report in the *Manchester Courier*, dated 29 September 1884 (below), described the club as a "four-year-old organisation". This is the first contemporary account to date the club's creation.

NEWTON HEATH (L.Y.R.) ASSOCIATION FOOTBALL CLUB. Hon. Sec., Mr. J. E. Elliott, 219, Droylesden-road, Newton Heath.

This four-year-old organisation seems to be in a very thriving condition since it boasts this season of "a better class of fixtures than ever, and a few good acquisitions" in the shape of new playing members, the gross total of which now reaches about 40. The best of the fixtures are those with Blackburn Olympic (second), Greenheys, Heywood, Manchester, and Oughtrington Park.

The article was written by the *Courier's* respected football columnist, "Dribbler", and was most likely based on information supplied to him by the Newton Heath secretary (club secretaries also supplied newspapers with match reports during this period). The newspaper appears to have been fastidious about its accuracy, and was always quick to print corrections, so it's worth noting that no correction to this article appeared in subsequent weeks. Certainly, the result of the first recorded game, a 6-0 defeat away to Bolton Wanderers reserves, suggests that the club were new to the association game.

On 27 November Manchester Arcadians fielded two teams. One side, which featured captain Percy Glass and brother Herbert, played Clarence Association while another played St Mark's at Longsight. A match report called them "somewhat deficient in combined play", a description that could also have applied to the region as a whole.

But football had at least laid down its roots in Manchester as a working man's game. And at its centre was the district of West Gorton.

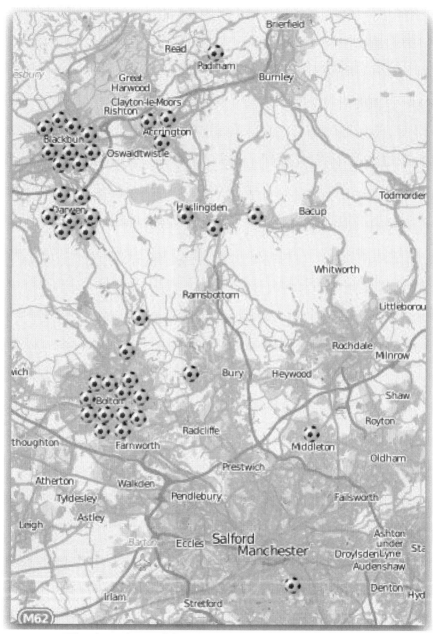

The location of football clubs for the inaugural
Lancashire FA Challenge Cup in 1878-79

The first association sides in the Manchester area

Date	Name	Home Ground	Origins
Oct-Nov 1875	Manchester Association	Moss Side	Probably formed by gentlemen players who had moved to area
Mar 1876	Broughton Wasps	Lower Broughton	Offshoot of rugby club
1877	Birch	Longsight CC	Offshoot of rugby club
1878	Hurst	Ashton-under-Lyne	Probably connected to Hurst Mills
1878	Manchester Association Wanderers	Whalley Range	Merger of Manchester Association & Manchester Wanderers
Apr 1879	Birch FC (2nd team)	Rusholme (possibly Birchfields Park)	Offshoot of rugby club
Apr 1879	Cheetham FC (1st team)	Tetlow Fold, Cheetham Hill	Offshoot of rugby club
Aug 1879	Middleton	Middleton	
Sep 1880	Manchester Arcadians	Moston Lane, Harpurhey	
13 Nov 1880	St Mark's	Longsight, near Belle Vue	Church of England
20 Nov 1880	Newton Heath	Newton Heath	L&Y Railway carriage works team
27 Nov 1880	Clarence Association	Tame Valley, Stalybridge	Possibly Clarence Mill works team

CHAPTER 2

THE HISTORY OF WEST GORTON

Rather annoyingly for any fan of the club, the story of Manchester City FC does not begin within the boundaries of the city at that time. It starts in the neighbouring township of Gorton, which was still mainly pasture land when the railways arrived in the 1840s. Manchester – the world's first industrial city – had witnessed staggering growth over the preceding decades. Its population rose from 22,481 in 1773 to 235,507 in 1841, driven by a cotton industry that had enjoyed a 40-fold sales increase over just half a century (an average growth of 7.7% per year).

Manchester was also becoming the hub of the new railway industry. In 1842 the Sheffield, Ashton-under-Lyne and Manchester railway opened two stations – Gorton and Hyde Road – priming that area for the type of growth that is nowadays only associated with China. John Ashbury's giant railway carriage works – which covered 11½ acres – had already opened just north of the railway line in Openshaw in 1841, and in 1846 industrialisation came to the eastern side of Gorton when work began on a depot for the new railway, dubbed the "Gorton Tank". The man who masterminded its construction, Richard Peacock, then teamed up with German engineer Charles Beyer to build steam locomotives. In 1854 the Beyer Peacock company began work on the Gorton Foundry, on land just south of Gorton Tank.

A year later another station, Ashbury's, opened between Gorton station and Ardwick Junction. Named after the carriage works' owner John Ashbury (it's still the only Manchester station named after a person who isn't a monarch) the station opened up the green fields to the south for development. This area, called Gorton Brook, would soon be known by another name: West Gorton.

By 1857 the population had grown from a handful to around

2,000 and the area had become home to extensive iron, chemical, cotton and paper works. Six years later West Gorton's population had more than doubled, and with construction now underway on Samuel Brooks's Union Iron works, it was set to grow even more. So in 1863 the Gorton Local Board was created and charged with the enormous task of dealing with the area's health and sanitation problems.

Where There's Muck...

The phrase "where there's muck there's money" was already in common usage in England by this time, and in West Gorton there was certainly plenty of both. A letter to the *Manchester Courier*, dated February 1866, detailed the appalling state of the roads in the area. Clowes Street, where St Mark's church was built a few months earlier, was dubbed "Slough-street" on account of its swamp-like conditions. The clearly-irate author also remarked,

> "No town in Lancashire, or even the black country,
> Staffordshire, can be found streets in a more
> abominable state of filth and mud than the roads are
> in Gorton".

In a time long before building codes the letter also noted that "the township is notorious for its jerry buildings". Indeed, West Gorton's Union Baptist Chapel actually fell down due to shoddy workmanship during this period, while in February 1875 the *Pall Mall Gazette* noted that some houses in the area had been constructed with "the least possible number of bricks", while "the fittings were almost always misfits, the doors and windows loose, and the doors easily pierced by the strong winds".

However, in the mighty Cottonopolis few tasks remained undone for long. Between 1830 and 1860 1,090 of the city's streets had been paved and sewered, and it wasn't long before Gorton's muddy problem was dealt with. By February 1866 tenders had been received for a main sewer for Clowes Street, and by the end of the year it was no longer dubbed "Slough

Street" after it was paved and flagged. Indeed, despite its teething problems, life in West Gorton was still an improvement on other industrialised areas of Manchester. In June 1866 the medical officer for Gorton and Openshaw, Mr J Brown, remarked of the area's inhabitants,

> "Their wages were good, but they were generally improvident. There were no nuisances of any magnitude".

At this time West Gorton shared few characteristics with the neighbouring city of Manchester which, in 1860, had 1,646 beerhouses, 485 public houses and 404 brothels (and just 617 police officers). At a 1867 Parliamentary inquiry into the city's boundaries, one witness declared that West Gorton "consists largely of workpeople employed at Beyers, and other large works, and not Manchester workpeople". The influx of male iron workers had another affect on West Gorton's demographics. In 1861 the city of Manchester had 97,420 female inhabitants but only 87,618 male. This reflected employment practices in the cotton mills, where typically around two-thirds of workers were female. In contrast, in the districts of Gorton and Openshaw – where iron works employees were exclusively male – 9,409 of its residents were men but only 9,112 were women.

The Great Distress

Gorton's booming iron industry was initially immune from the recessions that sporadically hit Manchester, including one created by the outbreak of the American Civil War in 1861. The severe cotton shortage it caused resulted in mass lay-offs at mills, sparking riots in the cotton districts east of Manchester such as Stalybridge and Ashton in 1863. West Gorton remained free from such unrest, with the well-paid employees of the Manchester, Sheffield and Lincolnshire (MSL) Railway even donating funds for Gorton's hard-hit mill workers. West Gorton was also less affected by the recession of 1868, which again saw rioting erupt in surrounding areas.

Contrary to common perception, a welfare system did exist in Victorian England – albeit a limited one. In Gorton it was administered by the Local Board, which granted payments to those who were unable to work. The area also had its "benefit cheats", with local newspapers running stories of people prosecuted for claiming unemployment payments despite being in work. But in the winter of 1878 Gorton's welfare system buckled under the force of a savage nationwide depression called the Great Distress. A report in the *Manchester Times* on 28 December 1878 detailed the devastation it brought to Gorton.

> "Organisations for dealing with the prevailing
> distress are extending from Manchester to its
> suburbs. In Gorton, where the population belongs
> almost exclusively to the working classes, the
> closing of the steelworks and reductions in the
> number of employes (sic) at some of the ironworks
> have, in conjunction with other causes, caused
> extraordinary hardship, and in some cases
> destitution among the people. A number of people
> have therefore formed themselves into a relief
> committee for this district, and they invite
> subscriptions which may be sent to Mr W H Wright,
> Church Inn, West Gorton; Mr E J Reynolds, 50,
> Cromwell-street, or any other member of the
> committee. Among their operations is the
> establishment and maintenance of a soup kitchen on
> premises attached to the Church Inn, Clowes-
> street."

According to the *Manchester Evening News*, the number of applications to Gorton's Poor Law guardians jumped from 228 on 7 October 1878 to 741 on 10 January 1879. The total receiving outdoor relief had risen from 1,966 to 4,183 – around

13% of the population. Added to the 1,592 in the workhouse it meant that nearly one in five people in Gorton were destitute.

The Gorton relief committee was soon in full swing helping more than 300 applicants a night. In the week ending 23 December, 600 gallons of soup, 1,100lbs of bread and five tons of coal were distributed. And, because this was Britain, large quantities of loose tea were also handed out.

By 1880, though, prosperity was returning to the area. Beyer Peacock, which sold just 66 locomotives in the year of the Distress compared to 161 three years earlier, was now back to full production. In September the *Gorton Reporter* noted that the "state of trade at Beyer Peacock is so good at present" that the firm would be unhappy at the loss of production caused by the upcoming annual week's holiday. Three years later the firm was making 181 locomotives a year, business elsewhere in Gorton was thriving, and unemployment rates were low.

By this time the rapid expansion of the area had ended. West Gorton now had a population of over 10,000, living mainly in tightly-packed rows of terraced houses on properly paved streets and with good sanitation. New religious bodies had arrived, including the Union Chapel, which had opened an impressive new church on Clowes Street in 1876. Out of the churches sprang new community organisations, including mothers' meetings set up in 1877 by the Anglican vicar's 24-year-old daughter, Georgina Connell, and the men's meetings established by her elder sister, Anna, in 1879. Both were held in St Mark's new church hall, which was opened in 1878 on Hyde Road. This was now a bustling thoroughfare, offering an array of shops, street goods and public houses. Gorton was also becoming a national transport hub after Belle Vue station opened in 1875. It offered express trains to London, and many other destinations, from its four spacious platforms. The area could also boast a literary society, a Mechanics Institute, a philharmonic orchestra, bands and choirs, an art night school, an array of social clubs and two thriving savings banks.

Indeed, by 1880 West Gorton was in danger of becoming respectable.

Gorton in the 1880s: What Life Was Like

If modern-day people stepped back in time to 1880s West Gorton the first thing to strike them would be the smell. The acrid smoke spewing out from the many iron foundries, chemical works and passing steam locomotives, combined with the tons of horse manure that dropped onto the streets each day, would produce a stench almost unimaginable today. With an ever-present thick blanket of smog cutting out all sunshine, health was a constant worry. Gorton's yearly death rate of around 25 per 1,000, although close to the national average, was nearly three times today's figure. Not surprisingly, bronchitis was the biggest killer followed by scarlet fever and tuberculosis. This was also an age before vaccinations and antibiotics, meaning that even a dose of the measles or a gashed knee could prove fatal.

Democracy was limited, with less than one in ten adults enfranchised. Women couldn't vote and men were only eligible if they paid local rates of £12 a year (six weeks' wages for a skilled iron worker). Even William Beastow, a member of the Gorton Local Board, inadvertently lost the vote briefly in 1879 after he discovered his landlord had not paid his rates in full.

In fact, Gorton in 1880 shared many characteristics with feudalism. On the eastern side of Gorton, Richard Peacock was every inch the local squire, keeping a paternal eye on his vassals from his Gorton Hall stately home. His high-tech plant was able to build a steam locomotive in a day, and Peacock used much of the vast wealth it produced for philanthropic acts such as the building of a new Unitarian church and providing free teas for the elderly. In contrast to the practical paternalism emanating from Beyer Peacock was Ashbury's carriage works. Following the death of its founder, John Ashbury, in 1866 the company was run by his nephew, engineer Thomas Ashbury. John Ashbury's only son, James, had long left the polluted air of Manchester while recovering from childhood illness (and found fame as a yachtsman, arranging and competing in the first America's Cup in 1871). He had taken with him the bulk of his father's £400,000 wealth (approximately £220million in today's money), and with Ashbury's now a public limited company, no individual from the firm exercised significant influence locally.

Work and Pay

West Gorton, though, was dominated by Samuel Brooks's Union Iron works, the world's leading maker of machinery for cotton mills, which had 700-900 employees. Work there was tough, dirty and often dangerous. Its employees worked a 54-hour week (reduced to 53 hours in April 1891) from 6am to 4pm Monday to Friday plus a half-day Saturday.

Workers were entitled to only one week's annual holiday, called Wakes Week, which was set to the first Saturday in September. Bank holidays were problematical. In August 1883 two Union Iron employees, David Vester and John Adshead, were each sentenced to two months hard labour after a dispute over a bank holiday escalated into violence. A Union Iron employee had been dismissed after he, along with other employees, took the bank holiday off without permission. Vester and Adshead, who both lived in West Gorton, were convicted of assaulting the man who had replaced the sacked worker. The incident appears to have been part of a long-running dispute over holidays. During the trial Brooks revealed that over the previous 20 years he "had been repeatedly annoyed in this way and had, in consequence to discharge men and engage others". Strikes frequently broke out at Ashbury's, and usually resulted in strikers being brought before the courts. In July 1885 Eli Hewitt, a unionised worker at the carriage works who had been locked-out, was fined 40 shillings for intimidating a strike-breaker, appropriately, in a railway carriage. Hewitt had called the man a "knobstick" and warned, "Mind that th'art spotted; bear in mind th'art a marked man".

Conditions inside the iron works posed another threat. In September 1885 a Union Iron labourer was left permanently disabled after an iron ball and hook smashed into his head. He sued under the Employers' Liability Act and was awarded £124 16s compensation, exactly three years' wages. Five years later an even more shocking accident took place when 13-year-old George Haughton inadvertently rested his hand on a leather strap that worked a grindstone. The strap was attached to a pulley, which pulled him into the shafting. His injuries were described as "shocking" and Haughton died soon afterward.

But the work was at least well paid. According to Peter Mathias's *The First Industrial Nation*, wages in British urban areas increased 60% in real terms between 1860-1900. The increasingly unionised iron workers were among the biggest beneficiaries. While labourers typically earned around 16 shillings a week, skilled iron workers took home between 40 to 50 shillings a week – roughly double what most mill workers received. In fact, this period marks the beginning of upward mobility among sections of the working class, with some iron workers becoming part of a group that came to be known as the "aristocracy of labour".

Employees of East Manchester's booming railway industry also shared a heightened social status compared to workers in many other industries. According to Jack Simmons's *The Railways of Britain*, a work-culture centered around the concept of duty was the norm. Indeed, in 1887 MSLR employees offered to forgo a day's wages to help meet the cost of a rail accident in Hexthorpe, Yorkshire, an offer that was declined by the company's directors. Subsidised accommodation, called railway cottages, helped push up the standard of living of railway employees to the point where money could be put aside. In March 1880 Bishop Fraser revealed that MSLR employees had £80,000 deposited in savings accounts, the equivalent of £33million today.

There was no income tax in Victorian England, and with a terraced house costing just 4 to 5 shillings a week to rent (home ownership for working people was unheard of in those days) it meant that West Gorton's workers generally had enough cash to spare for the odd luxury – as long as they were healthy enough to work.

Crime and Punishment

Crime was a constant issue in Manchester, as it was in any city. In Gorton it centred around property, drink and family, but local newspapers do not convey any sense that it was perceived as getting out of control. Domestic assault was one of the most commonly tried offences, probably stemming from cramped living conditions (the average household contained 5-6 people) and the fact that divorce was nearly impossible to obtain. In July 1880 William Swallow was charged with attempting to murder his mother and step-father in Robert Street, West Gorton, and the same month an attempted wife-murder scandalised the area. Gortonions were also gripped by the letter-writing campaign of an Ashton man who chose to be remanded in Belle Vue Gaol rather than pay maintenance for the wife he detested (the man claimed he had been an "ass" for marrying the woman but had now turned into a "stubborn mule"). In fact, the consequences of being stuck with a partner you hated appears to have been one of the biggest talking points in 1880s life, something that the press were not slow to pick up on. Virtually every newspaper edition contained at least one story of domestic violence. In May 1886, for instance, the *Manchester Times* ran a story under the headline "Setting fire to a wife" above another story headlined "Shooting a wife in bed". Both involved Manchester men.

The issue of abortion also hit the headlines on occasions. In April 1875 Alfred Heap, a 33-year-old druggist living in Gorton Lane, was hanged for the murder of a 26-year-old West Gorton woman after an abortion he performed resulted in her death. Although contraceptive devices were available during this period (the invention of vulcanised rubber in the 1840s led to the manufacture of artificial condoms and diaphragms), knowledge about how to acquire and use them was not publicly available. This began to change two years later after an attempt to ban a book on birth control, called *Fruits of Philosophy*, resulted in it becoming a best-seller (according to one report nationwide sales of the book increased from 700 copies a year to 90,000 in a fortnight following the court case).

Another source of sensationalist headlines from the mid-1870s was youth gang fighting dubbed "scuttling", though it wasn't until 1884 that a problem on Gorton's streets was reported. That year saw a spate of "scuttling" cases, a term that appears to be a catch-all for a variety of offences. One violent attack took place near Ashbury's works and appears to be connected to a bitter year-long strike by unionised smiths that took place there. Another saw three young Catholic men assaulted on the way to

Gorton's monastery and likely reflected the ethnic tensions in Gorton at that time. The number of "scuttling" cases dropped dramatically in 1885 after two young West Gorton men were sentenced to 12 months hard labour, and by 1890 police superintendent Bent told the Gorton Local Board that

> "After 'a good deal of inquiry' he was quite satisfied
> that scuttling, in the proper sense of the term, did
> not exist, nor had it existed for some time in Gorton.
> He did not believe there was a township anywhere
> of the same population so free from real crime as
> Gorton."

Leisure Time

Not surprisingly, considering the length of the working week, leisure time was limited. But higher than average wages did provide West Gortonians with plenty of ways to unwind, particularly with the giant Belle Vue pleasure gardens on their doorstep. For sixpence admission this Victorian "Disneyland" offered a large zoo and gardens, refreshment rooms that could accommodate up to 3,000 visitors, as well as an array of attractions including sports contests, brass band competitions, spectacular firework displays and floodlit ballroom dancing. In January 1879 – at the depth of the bitterly cold winter of the Great Distress – Belle Vue provided one of the most wondrous spectacles of the era. After the vast frozen artificial lake inside the gardens froze over, floodlights "equal in power to 8,000 candles" were placed on top of a clock tower on an island in the middle of the lake. According to the *Manchester Times*

> "Probably 2,000 persons were skating on the ice,
> the white surface of which added much by
> reflection to the intense brilliancy of the light, and
> showed the shadows of the skaters, and of the trees
> on the island with the sharpness and the blackness
> of a shadow pantomime".

ZOOLOGICAL GARDENS,
BELLE VUE, MANCHESTER.

Clock Tower and Lake

An early 1900s postcard showing the lake where 2,000 people skated. Floodlit dancing also took place beside the lake.

The sight would have been a particularly spectacular one in view of the semi-darkness that late Victorian Manchester was normally cloaked in. For roughly two-thirds of the year West Gorton's residents would have walked to work before sunrise, along cobbled streets lit by dim gas lamps. Their homes were candle-lit and, given the high cost of candles, would be shadowy places. In an era long before radio and television, the lack of entertainment in the home would hardly lighten the gloom..

Little wonder then that the area's public houses enjoyed good trade. They would have stood out as bright beacons of cheer, offering warmth, companionship and relaxation. The exclusively male workforce of the iron and rail industries, coupled with their relatively high renumeration, meant that few West Gorton wives worked outside the home – unlike most working-class women who did. That freed men from most household chores, providing more opportunity to "rehydrate" down the pub. For many they were a centre of social life, and the home to a variety of pastimes. These ranged from skittles to vegetable-growing contests, including a cucumber show held at the Church Inn on Clowes Street in the summer of 1880, in which St Mark's church official Edwin Reynolds won third place.

The fact that a Church warden was taking part in activities organised by a public house illustrated the ambivalence the Church had towards drink. Indeed, that year another St Mark's official, William Beastow, raised no objection to the opening of a new public house in the area during a Local Board meeting. Instead, religious and political organisations focused on providing alternatives to the attractions of the public house. For instance, the local Liberal Club offered billiards players the chance to practice that increasingly-popular pastime in a non-alcoholic environment, while a "reading and skittles" club operated off Clowes Street during the summer.

Gorton did not have a theatre, largely because of protests from religious groups. In June 1877 an application to open one in nearby Openshaw ran into fierce opposition from four local churches, who organised a 1,200-name petition. Presenting it to magistrates, Church education campaigner Thomas Chorlton declared that theatres "catered for a very low class of entertainment, and tended to foster a very low taste among young people" (there also may have been a dislike of the escapist nature of theatre within the Church, illustrated by Bishop Fraser's criticism of the acting profession in a speech later that year, in which he urged actors to instead engage in the "drama of life"). St Mark's was one of the churches that helped organise the petition, and its involvement reflected the growing concern of churches about "misuse" of leisure time by their parishioners as the working week shortened and income grew. The leisure activities of young men were a particular concern, and the church's attempts to address the issue would soon play a major role in the establishment of sport in the area.

The Origins of St Mark's Church

The first known church in West Gorton was a Zion Chapel, located near the eastern boundary on Gorton Lane, which was rented by Independent Dissenters. In 1861 the landlord put it up for sale, along with 14 cottages and a dwelling house. The following year, possibly unable to find a buyer, the chapel and its adjoining schoolroom were rented to the Church of England for £36 a year, paid for by locomotive builder Charles Beyer. In February 1862 a new church called St Mark's began services there. It was part of the parish of St James, and for the first three years most services were conducted by the curate of St James, Rev. Richard Adams.

The first baptism was performed on 18 November 1862. Curiously, church records reveal that two months later Adams performed a staggering 73 baptisms on one day. Three weeks later, on 18 February 1863, he performed 66 baptisms. Records of nearby churches reveal nothing close to this scale. Assuming the records are not the result of clerical error the numbers pose something of a mystery, particularly as many parents baptised several of their children at one time. On 22 January, for instance, carpenter Richard Pattinson and his wife Margaret had seven of their children baptised. It may be the baptisms were performed for the children of newly-arrived building workers who were constructing the Union Iron works. It's also possible that this was an early example of the modern-day practice of parents baptising children so that they can attend a local church school. At this time St Mark's school, which had been established by Rev. Adams, was teaching 360 pupils a week and was the only day school in West Gorton.

By April 1864 West Gorton contained 813 houses, with 69 new ones being built (probably for the workers of Union Iron which had opened that August). St Mark's was now ready to expand, and on 30 April the foundation stone of a new church was laid on land donated by Colonel Clowes. Costing £2,800, it was initially planned to hold 510 worshippers, just over double the capacity of the rented chapel. A new school was also built beside the church, and both were paid for by two of the owners of Beyer Peacock: its co-founder Charles Beyer and shareholder Henry Robertson, a railway engineer who was then the Liberal MP for Shrewsbury, who each donated £1,000.

Suicide at St Mark's

The new church would have placed a huge burden on the three hard-pressed clergymen of the St James parish. Its rector, Rev. Richard Basnett, and his two curates, Rev. Richard Adams and Rev. John Kennedy, now had to manage a major building project as well as run two churches and schools. So the death of Rev. Basnett in October 1864, and the month's wait for the appointment of a new rector, likely pushed the Gorton church to near breaking-point. That winter the 31-year-old Adams stood down as curate, for unknown reasons. Two new clergymen, Richard Tomlins, chaplain at Belle Vue Gaol, and Rev. Frederick Lullemand began taking services at St Mark's, and Kennedy also performed a baptism there. On 2 March 1865 Adams received his parting gifts from parishioners, consisting of a "handsome" timepiece, a silver pen and pencil and a gold bronze inkstand.

Two days later the parish suffered another loss, but this time in tragic circumstances. On 6 March newspapers reported the suicide of 35-year-old Rev. Kennedy. A doctor and police officer, who had been called to his lodgings, broke open his locked bedroom door and found him dead in bed. According to the *Courier*, his "throat was cut nearly from ear to ear, and there was a tremendous gash 12 inches long, with a smaller one three inches long, across the stomach". Mysteriously, the newspaper claimed the 35-year-old Kennedy "had been labouring under great excitement during a few days past, in consequence of recent difficulties". Another newspaper report, hinting at financial irregularities, claimed the suicide was "in consequence, apparently, of pecuniary embarrassment". This might explain why a report on the laying of the foundation stone from 2 May was unusually vague about the final cost of the project, stating that it was between £3000-£4,000.

SUICIDE BY A CLERGYMAN AT GORTON.—On Saturday the Rev. John Kennedy, curate of Gorton, committed suicide at his lodgings, at the house of Mr. Johnson. He had been labouring under great excitement during a few days past, in consequence of recent difficulties. On Sunday morning, not making his usual appearance, the people of the house knocked at his bedroom door, which was bolted. Having done this several times in vain, the door was broken open ; and Dr. Brown, who was attending deceased, and police-constable Rogers, upon entering, found him lying on his left side on the floor, in his shirt and stockings, with a pillow under his head. His throat was cut nearly from ear to ear, and there was a tremendous gash 12 inches long, with a smaller one three inches long, across the stomach. A razor was lying near his left arm. He was unmarried, and about 35 years of age.

The Manchester Courier's account of Kennedy's suicide

Adams continued performing services at St Mark's following the suicide, and between March and July 1865 five clergymen officiated at baptisms: Adams, new rector George Philpot (who was appointed on 14 November 1864), Tomlins, Joseph Kun and Herbert Williams. On 13 August another clergyman is recorded as performing baptism: Rev. Arthur Connell, who became the rector of St Mark's for the next three decades. On 6 November 1865, a week after St Mark's 640-seat church was consecrated,

Connell was licensed to its incumbency. In July 1866 he was appointed the first rector of the newly-formed St Mark's parish.

The Railway Rector

The new head of St Mark's was a man of unquestioning belief in the righteousness of his cause – and the falseness of other religions. Connell was born in Mallow, Ireland around 1822, a member of the Anglo-Protestant ruling class. At 29, married with daughters aged five and three, Connell enrolled at St Aidan's College, Birkenhead, where he studied theology. His choice of college was an unorthodox one. St Aidan's was established and run by the autocratic and controversial figure of Joseph Baylee, an ardent millennialist who believed that Armageddon was approaching. Before the world's end, Baylee predicted that a "catastrophe" would take place in 1897 (incidentally, the year Connell would resign from the Church on health grounds). This would be followed in 1927 by the "restoration" of "purified Jews" to Palestine, that is, Jews who had converted to Christianity. This Restorationist movement was an early form of what would become known as "Christian Zionism", an evangelical movement that believed the return of Jews to the Holy Land was necessary for biblical prophesies to be fulfilled.

Connell would go on to be described as an "earnest evangelical" in one obituary, and at evangelicalism's core was the concept that believers had an obligation to save non-believers from eternal hell. A contemporary of Connell's, influential US evangelist Dwight Moody, likened his calling to a sea rescue mission. "God has given me a lifeboat," Moody insisted, "and said 'Moody, save all you can.'" It's likely that Connell had a similar mindset on leaving St Aidan's in 1856.

On 1 July 1856 he was appointed to the curacy of Shankhill Parish Church, Lurgan, Northern Ireland. The following June he became Assistant-Curate at Tullylish Parish Church in Gilford, County Down. The area was a hotbed of evangelicalism which, in March 1858, included a project to send out bibles to the 1.5 million Gaelic-speaking Irish (23% of Ireland's population). Connell was particularly interested in the conversion of Jews, whom he called a "trodden down and afflicted people". In December 1864 the *Leeds Intelligencer* reported that he promoted a scheme in Harrogate to send bibles to what he called the "fallen race" of Jews. Behind the scheme was the London Society for Promoting Christianity among the Jews, an early Restorationist organisation. Connell's evangelistic interest in the plight of Jews, along with his choice of college, suggest that he too may have been a Restorationist with end-time beliefs. The titles of Connell's three published works – *The Triumphant Saviour*, *The Great Conflict* and *The Heavenly Multitude* – do have an apocalyptic flavour. However until these works materialise, it is impossible to say for sure.

Connell's career was also closely tied to the spread of the railways. The start of his ministry in Northern Ireland coincided with the building of the Banbridge railway, which brought industrial development to his parish of Tullylish. In 1859 he became curate at Christ Church, Harrogate (after turning down an offer from Tullylish parishioners to match his pay rise), an area that saw large-scale redevelopment following the opening of Harrogate central railway station in 1862. Extensive enlargements were also carried out at Christ Church during his time there, and it was probably his experience in fast-expanding parishes that made him an ideal candidate for St Mark's.

West Gorton would have been an horrendous sight for many during this period, a patchwork of building sites and mud that had spewed out around the new railway lines. But for Arthur Connell it represented business as usual. And for a clergyman from Northern Ireland, Gorton's ethnic divide would be more familiar still.

Protestants v Papists

The newly-developed West Gorton was an overwhelmingly Anglican area. In 1864 Gorton's MP estimated that at least 530 out of 800 dwellings (66%) were occupied by members of the Church of England. That's a surprisingly high figure considering that the Church of England accounted for just 38% of the churches and 45% of the seating room in Manchester during this period. Indeed West Gorton's Primitive Methodist chapel had only 70 worshippers while the Baptist Union Chapel, which opened on Clowes Street in 1862, had just 30. West Gorton was also an almost exclusively Protestant area, not altogether surprising considering it contained roads with names such as "Cromwell Street". In stark contrast to this were the back streets around Gorton Lane, to the east of the parish boundary. That area had become a "Little Ireland" and was home to a Catholic monastery that boasted an average congregation of 350 (the ethnic divide was still very much in place two decades later, with the 1881 census revealing that less than 1% of West Gorton's population were Irish while in some of the streets off Gorton Lane they accounted for around 80% of householders). Living conditions in the Irish community were poor. In 1866 the medical officer for Gorton and Openshaw, Mr J Brown, declared that the "overcrowding and filth" of the district "was almost entirely confined to the Irish, who formed a large proportion of the residents".

The Irish at this time were popularly viewed as being lower on the evolutionary hierarchy than Anglo-Saxons. Cartoons in Punch magazine portrayed them as having bestial, ape-like or demonic features. Some scientists ranked them low down on the "Index of Nigrescence" while in 1857 historian, novelist and Anglican clergyman Charles Kingsley referred to the large number of "human chimpanzees" in Ireland. These attitudes appear to be reflected in Brown's comments about their poor living conditions. He observed that the Irish "as a rule totally disregarded all the laws of health".

Manchester had become home to a huge number of Irish immigrants over the preceding decades. By 1846 it was estimated that 40,000 had settled there, 15% of the city's population. Those numbers swelled during the Great Famine of 1845-50, which caused an estimated one million deaths. The famine also resulted in around a million people emigrating from Ireland, bringing with them bitterness towards British rule. The anger found a home in the Irish Republican Brotherhood, a secret society dedicated to armed uprising that was created in 1858. Their rebellion, called the Fenian Rising, came in February 1867. Although soundly crushed a month later, the aftershock was felt in Gorton that September when a police officer was shot dead during an ambush of a horse-drawn police van carrying two members of the Irish Republican Brotherhood from Belle Vue Gaol. The ensuing court case – dubbed the "Manchester Outrage" – saw three men hanged for murder, though many believed them innocent.

A contemporary drawing of the Fenian attack on the police van

The incident provoked a wave of anti-Irish feeling. In Gorton, where the foundations for a giant Franciscan monastery had been laid on Gorton Lane a year earlier, the suspicion that its Irish community supported the uprising would have led to increased tension. But it was in Manchester's hard-hit cotton districts that anger spilled over. Resentment had already built up towards impoverished Irish immigrants, who were willing to work for less pay than British-born workers. But the severe cotton shortage brought about by the outbreak of the American Civil War in 1861 had devastated Manchester's cotton industry, and turned some areas into tinder-boxes. In May 1868 anti-Irish rioting erupted in the cotton districts of Ashton, Stalybridge and Duckinfield. They were known as the "Murphy Riots", named after Orange Order supporter William Murphy, who toured these deprived areas preaching about Catholicism's evils. Murphy was originally a Roman Catholic who converted to the Church of England (a fact that probably disqualified him from becoming a member of the Orange Order), and his lectures reflected a zealotry often associated with converts. In one of his most inflammatory speeches, Murphy declared that "every Popish priest was a murderer, a cannibal, a liar, and a pickpocket". Arthur Connell, author of *The Great Conflict*, did not shy away from this ethnic and cultural battle. He had already made his views on Catholicism clear during his time in Northern Ireland. In a lecture given at the Tullylish church in 1858 Connell declared that "the history of Roman Catholicism afforded the most unquestionable evidence in proof of Romanism being in direct antagonism to the Word of God", adding that there was not one of the ten commandments that the Catholic Church was "not guilty of violating".

By 1869 ethnic troubles flared elsewhere in Manchester. English Anglicans, alarmed at Prime Minister William Gladstone's plans to disestablish the Irish Church, took to the streets to protest, and were sometimes met with violence from groups of Irish immigrant counter-protesters. According to a letter in the *Manchester Courier* on 5 July 1869, the wearing of blue was "sufficient to endanger the wearer's life" during a Protestant rally at the Pomona Gardens. The letter's author claimed that Protestant demonstrators were set upon by Romanists after the rally, who smashed six windows of a bus.

In November 1869 Connell invited a colleague of Murphy's, William Touchstone, to deliver a lecture entitled "The life and times of William III" at St Mark's school. Introducing the lecture, Connell declared (to cries of "hear, hear") that "in the present day we had Jesuits within the Church and we had Jesuits without the Church, jesuistically planning and plotting again to subordinate England to the see of Rome". He added:

> "The minds of the people were beginning to be
> enlightened with respect to the dark, deadly,
> treacherous designs of the Romanists and Romish
> aggression".

Connell was referring to the "Papal Aggression" of 1850, in which the Vatican restored a Catholic hierarchy in Britain. He shared a commonly held belief in Protestant circles that this was part of a plot to take over the country and deprive the British people of the freedoms granted to them by the Protestant Reformation. During his lecture Touchstone emphasised this point.

> "Romanism was diametrically opposed to the
> liberty of the subject," he declared. "Popery being
> then, as it is now, and ever would be, dangerous to
> the State".

It was precisely this message that sparked the riots that swept the cotton districts a year earlier. Indeed, Touchstone had spoken at some of those same Orange Order meetings as Murphy. The fact that similar violence did not erupt in Gorton may be largely down to economic reasons. Although West Gorton was suffering the effects of a recession at this time, the local iron works — and their largely Protestant workforce — were not nearly as badly hit as the cotton mills of Ashton, Stalybridge and Duckinfield.

William Murphy suffered an early death in 1872, probably the result of being savagely beaten by a mob of Irishmen a year earlier in Whitehaven, Cumberland. Anti-Popery began to wane in the ensuing years, so much so that in 1877 the future Anglican Bishop of Liverpool declared that "many now-a-days regard the subject of Popery as a bore". Among Anglican clergymen, however, their opposition to Popery turned inwards, leading to a prolonged civil war over "Papish" ritualistic practices in the Church. This dispute resulted in the imprisonment of several

Anglican clergymen for performing rituals that had been outlawed by the 1874 Public Worship Regulation Act. Among them was Rev. Sidney Green, rector of St John's in Miles Platting, who was imprisoned for 20 months in 1880. Connell vigorously supported the sentence, telling Manchester's Bishop Fraser in 1883 that "it had preserved the Church of England from becoming a wreck".

Connell was also a vocal supporter of the Orange Order. At a meeting of the Duke of Lancaster Lodge in November 1884, he declared that the Order "identified themselves with the onward movements of truth, the bloodless triumph of the cross of Christ, and the maintenance and preservation of our civil, religious, and political liberties". The Orange Order was well-represented in his parish. The secretary of St Mark's Penny Bank in 1880, Thomas Neilson, was also District Treasurer in the Manchester District Loyal Orange Lodge. And according to research by Manchester Orange Order archivist Jack Greenald, Connell's first curate at St Mark's, Rev. Charles Fenwick Ward, was likely to have been a member. Greenald also discovered that at a ceremony to mark Connell's 21st year at St Mark's in December 1886, two of the four clergymen who gave addresses were Orangemen.

Sectarianism remained an issue in Gorton for some time. In June 1893 Connell was accused of "the lowest form of sectarian bigotry" by Liberal London weekly newspaper *Truth* after he withdrew St Mark's pupils from a school parade because they weren't allowed to march at the front.

Worlds Apart

But if the world of late 19th century West Gorton appears alien to us, consider what the Rev. Connell would make of present-day Manchester. While the behaviour and attire of many modern women would immediately bring the word "harlots" to his lips, the existence of a "gay village" where homosexuals openly display their sexuality would provoke profound shock. And the discovery that a Conservative Prime Minister was in favour of homosexual men marrying each other would likely lead the millennialist Connell to assume that a Biblical terror was soon be unleashed on this 21st century "city of Sodom".

SECTARIANISM IN GORTON.

To-day's *Truth* says:—An edifying exhibition of the lowest form of sectarian bigotry occurred last week at the opening of a new park in the Gorton Division of Manchester. In the demonstration on this occasion there was to be a procession of school children. The committee held a ballot to decide the order in which the schools should march, with the result that a Roman Catholic school drew the first place and a Nonconformist the second. Upon this, two clerics of the Established Church, the Revs. A. Connell and Birch Jones, sent word to the committee that if the children of the Establishment could not walk first they should not walk at all. A third Church school followed suit, with the result that the Church of England was not represented. There is a certain type of Anglican cleric who if invited to walk into heaven behind a Nonconformist would prefer to go in the opposite direction.

The report from June 1893

But then 19th century Manchester had strikingly different cultural values and norms to the current era. In March 1880 the six acts performing at the People's Music Hall each evening included Clifford and Franks, the "Comic Niggers" and H Daniels, the "Eccentric Nigger". Mothers routinely fed opium-based cough mixtures to their young children, which were sold in local druggist stores alongside morphine, laudanum and "Indian hemp" cannabis cigarettes – dubbed the Victorian "wonder-drug".

However, other aspects of 1880 society would be instantly recognisable. Britain was fighting a war in Afghanistan that year, as well as one against the Zulus in South Africa, though neither impacted directly on the lives of the vast majority. War was also a source of entertainment, with victorious Afghan War battles played out in the pages of boys' magazines and re-enacted – complete with fireworks – at Belle Vue's pleasure gardens (though Victorians would be shocked that in Britain's modern-day wars victories are not celebrated, nor defeats mourned).

But above all, 1880 Manchester was a city on the brink of great social and technological change. The start of the year saw the opening of the city's first telephone exchange. It marked the beginnings of the electrical age, which the following year would see the first plans for electric street lighting in Manchester. Millions of working men would soon become enfranchised – the product of the Manchester-led Chartist movement of the 1840s – while in Moss Side in September 1880 Christabel Pankhurst was born. Along with mother Emmiline Pankhurst she would later organise the first suffragette campaign from the Pankhurst's Manchester family home.

A stone's throw from the Pankhurt's home, the Rev. George Garrett, from the Anglican Christ Church in Moss Side, had invented the world's first self-propelled submarine. In February 1880 his 45ft long 30-tonne steam-powered *Resurgum II* was launched from Birkenhead, symbolising the spirit of innovation that abounded in Manchester. Garrett was also a good example of the city's entrepreneurial spirit, later selling submarines to the Greek government, and then to their deadly enemies, the Turks.

Despite Garrett's life being worthy of its own book (he was the only man in history to have been awarded the titles of English Reverend, Turkish Lord and US Corporal), this remarkable Mancunian has long been forgotten. But three miles east of the leafy opulence of Victorian Moss Side another Anglican clergyman was creating his own legacy. In November 1880 the earnest evangelical rector of St Mark's, West Gorton was helping lay the groundwork for a new era of spectator sport, appropriately beside the wonderland of the Belle Vue pleasure gardens. It marked Manchester's formal introduction to a social phenomenon that currently defines the city: its entry into the age of association football.

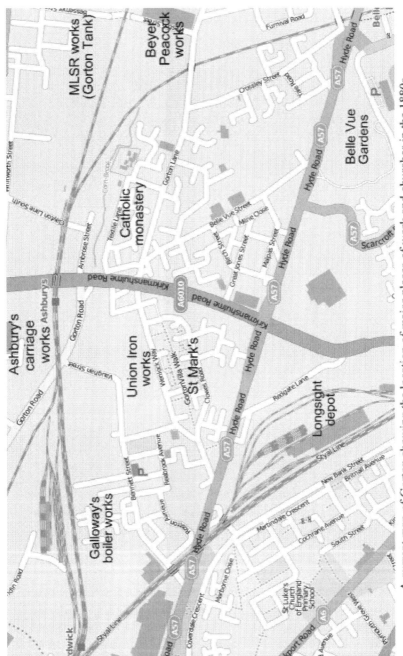

A current map of Gorton showing the location of major places of work and churches in the 1880s

Population growth in Gorton & Openshaw

Year	West Gorton	Gorton	Openshaw
1821			497
1830		1,604	
1831			838
1841		2,422	2,283
1851		4,476	3,759
1857	around 2,000		
1861	4,305 (parish)	9,897	8,623
May 1864	4,065 (813 houses + 69 being built)		
1867	About 6,000 ("broad estimate")		
1871	4,705	21,616	11,108
1877		in excess of 30,000	
1881		30-35,000	16,153
1883	11,188 (parish)	35,714	
1894-95	15,215	41,207	

What things cost in 1880
(£1 = 240d, 1 shilling = 12d)

Essential items	Cost
Rent of terraced house	4s-5s a week
Coal (1 kwt)	1s 3d
Paraffin (½ gallon)	3d
Soap (1lb)	2d
Food and drink	
Meat (1 lb)	1s 3d
Loaf of bread (2 lb)	3d
Vegetables (3 lb)	2d
Tea (½ lb)	1s
Sugar (2 lb)	5d
Clothes	
Tweed trousers	7s 6d
Tweed suit	21s
Boy's suit	1s 11d
Overcoat	30s
Boots	10s 6d
Pair of socks	10d
Non-essential items	
Pint of beer	3d
Pack of Woodbine cigarettes	1d
Newspaper	1d

Punishments for crimes committed in Gorton in 1880

Offence	Punishment
Sleeping out	caution
Wheeling coal wagon on footpath	caution
Threatening wife	Bound over for 6 weeks (£12 bonds)
Threatening wife because she was gambling	Bound over (£10 bond)
Obstructing footpath with wares	1s
Profane language	1s / 2s 1d
Allowing horse to stray	2s 6d
Failing to ensure child's school attendance	6d (+ 1s or 2s costs)
Fighting drunk	5s
Kicking wife	5s
Owning dog without a licence	5s
Drunk & lying on footpath	5s (+ 7s 6d costs or 14 days)
Drunk in charge of horse & cart	20s
Riding horse & cart while asleep	20s
Selling unsound meat	20s + costs

Punishments for serious crimes

Offence	Punishment
Theft of stockings from washing line (by male)	8 strokes of a birch rod
Theft of square from Union Iron	1 week custody
Wilful damage	1 month hard labour
Stealing flowers from Belle Vue Gardens	1 month hard labour
Failing to report for supervision & begging	2 months hard labour
Stealing boots from infant girl	3 months hard labour
Stealing half sovereign from girl in beer house	3 months hard labour
Assaulting police officer	6 months hard labour
Theft of £2 from surgeon by assistant	6 months hard labour

Source: *Gorton Reporter*

CHAPTER 3

THE BIRTH OF ST MARK'S FOOTBALL CLUB

The earliest record of team sport being played in Gorton was a match in July 1860 involving the Gorton Cricket Club, which appears to have been made up of gentlemen players. For the working men of the area organised sporting activity appears to have been confined to public holidays. On 7 September 1861, for instance, the *Manchester Times* revealed that the Wakes Week holiday Monday at Belle Vue included "old English holiday sports, such as football and dancing round the Maypole". With 30,000 people at the pleasure gardens that day the football may also have been played in front of a sizeable crowd (sadly, the *Manchester Times* report focused almost exclusively on a band contest, stating merely that the sports "were of the usual character").

But by the mid-1860s the first references to working people playing cricket began to appear. In May 1865 Gorton's second sports team – called Gorton Works after the Beyer Peacock foundry – appears in match reports.

Two years later St Mark's created its first sport team, a cricket club whose first game against St Barnabas church, Openshaw, was played on 22 June 1867. Match reports from this period illustrate the important role religious bodies played in the early development of team sport. For instance, at least seven of the 16 clubs listed in the *Manchester Courier* on 15 August 1867 had church connections. By the late 1860s team sport was flourishing in Gorton. In 1869 six cricket clubs sprang up in the area, while at least 30 Gorton sporting clubs were created between 1867 and November 1880 – the date of St Mark's first recorded game of association football. Rugby came to the area in 1877, when three new clubs were formed. It's possible that this was connected to the closure of Gorton's Working Men's Club that year. It had just 14 members (out of a population of more than

30,000) when it closed, and the creation of new rugby clubs may have represented a fresh approach to combating the attractions of the public house.

BAIRD-STREET WORKING MEN v. SALFORD TRINITY ALLIANCE.—Score: Working Men, 20 and 25; Trinity Alliance, 108.

BRADFORD FREE CHURCH v. ARDWICK.—Played on the ground of the former, and was decided in favour of the Ardwick in one innings. Score: Bradford, 48 and 37; Ardwick, 101.

CRAB-LANE UNION v. CRUMPSALL WORKING MEN.—Played at Crumpsall, and resulted in an easy victory for the Union. Score: Union, 74; Working Men, 24.

MANCHESTER AMICABLE v. HAWTHORN.—Played on the ground of the former. Score: Amicable, 63, and 41 for the loss of eight wickets; Hawthorn, 53 and 45.

PLYMOUTH-GROVE AND GROUND v. BRUNSWICK.—Played at Plymouth-grove, on the ground of the former, and resulted in a victory for Plymouth grove in one innings and 21 runs to spare. Score: Brunswick, 15 and 46; Plymouth-grove, 82.

STAVERT, ZIGOMALA, AND CO.'S EMPLOYES v. ST. CLEMENT'S.—Played at Ardwick. Score: St. Clement's, 21 and 20; Employés, 30 and 32.

ST. MATTHEW'S (HYDE-ROAD) v. ST. MARK'S (WEST GORTON).—Played at West Gorton. Score: St. Matthew's, 78; St. Mark's, 23 and 37.

ST. PHILIP'S (BRADFORD-ROAD) v. ST. JOHN'S (MILES PLATTING.—Played on the ground of the latter. Score: St. Philip's, 55; St. John's, 28, and 21 with two wickets to fall.

The Manchester Courier, 15 August 1867

Battle of the Sunday Schools

It's not clear whether the 1867 St Mark's side originated from the church or its schools. But in July 1872 reports of another cricket team, called St Mark's Sunday School, first appear. By June 1877 a local sporting rivalry between denominations had sprung up, with a side called West Gorton Union Sunday School now playing cricket. It was a rivalry that appears to have had a major bearing on the development of Manchester football.

Manchester's Sunday schools had witnessed dramatic growth

over the previous century. By 1880, the year of the 100th anniversary of the founding of the first Sunday school in Britain, there were 268 of them in the Greater Manchester area teaching 104,267 pupils, compared to just 2,826 pupils in 1785. A series of events marked the anniversary that year, prompting much debate about future development.

On 19 July 1880 the Manchester Sunday School Union, which represented non-conformist churches, held its centenary conference at Association Hall, Peter Street, home of the Manchester YMCA. In his opening address, president Rueben Spencer announced the need to expand the number of sporting clubs attached to their schools. According to the *Courier*

> "Beyond teaching in the moral sense, he would more largely develop the physical element of our Sunday-school life. He said most emphatically that wherever it was possible he would have the gymnasium, the cricket, football, reading and discussion clubs in connection with each Sunday school, so as to have it a centre of both moral and physical education. (Hear, hear)".

On 5 October the Church of England held its Sunday school centenary celebration, also at Association Hall. A succession of speakers warned that the Church had been losing ground to the non-conformists. One warned that non-conformity "was assuming gigantic proportions and gaining fresh ground", in large part because of the "wonderful machinery" of their Sunday schools. He noted that these schools were having "unequalled success in retaining elder scholars". Calling on the assembled clergymen to recognise the "existing abuses and defects" of their schools, he also called on them to utilise "supplementary aids out of school".

Arthur Connell was one of the clergymen in attendance that day. And on 6 November he listened to Bishop Fraser spell out an even more pressing concern facing the Church at that time: the problem of young men. In a keynote speech at Manchester

Cathedral (only his third "visitation" in a decade as bishop), Fraser revealed that over the previous 11 years only 14,050 young men had been confirmed into the Manchester Church compared to 73,754 young women. Fraser told the assembled clergymen that the increasing disparity indicated a "prevalence of the notion that the profession of religion is a thing for women rather than men". Young men who wanted to stay in the Church were "subjected to annoyances and ridicule", he said. The notion that religion was unmanly was one that the Church "must fight against with all the resources that are at our command", Fraser declared. It was a task that required "the ripest wisdom and maturest pastoral experience", and should "not to be delegated to the young curate or scripture-reader".

The evangelical Connell, a vocal supporter of the bishop's call for change, was not a man to shirk a challenge. That afternoon a new rugby club, called St Mark's Rovers, played its first recorded match against Lawn (possibly Audenshaw's Beech Lawn Cricket Club) at West Gorton. A week later a St Mark's association football side played their first match against Baptist of Macclesfield, the first recorded example of working men playing the code in Manchester.

St. Mark's Rovers (West Gorton) v. Lawn.—This match was played at West Gorton on Saturday, and resulted as follows:—St. Mark's, two tries, one touchdown, one touch-in-goal, and one dead ball; Lawn, one touch-in-goal.

A report of the St Mark's rugby side from 9 November 1880

The two St Mark's clubs played alternate Saturdays until 18 December, when both fielded teams. That suggests a degree of co-ordination on the part of the church, possibly with the intention of assessing the suitability and popularity of the two codes. The relative dangers of the two football codes was a subject debated in newspapers that winter, and earlier that month the mayor of Southampton had banned the playing of rugby following the death of a player. Considering the similarity of football and rugby back then it's also likely that some players turned out for both sides before settling on their preferred code. Indeed, later newspaper reports reveal that at least two early St Mark's footballers had switched to rugby.

The new St Mark's teams were a product of the "Muscular" Christianity movement, whose driving force was the desire to make Christianity more "manly". The game of football, according to historian Brian Dobbs, could not be better suited for the promotion of this task. It was

> "a game that exhausted boys before they could fall
> victims to vice and idleness, which at the same time
> instilled the manly virtues of absorbing and
> inflicting pain in about equal proportions, which
> elevated the team above the individual, which bred
> courage, loyalty and discipline".

The need to reinforce the parish's identity following changes to its boundaries might also have been a factor in the creation of the sports clubs. In March 1880 a new Anglican church opened 400 yards to the north-west of St Mark's. Costing £12,000, the imposing 12,600 sq ft St Benedict's was more than three times the size of St Mark's. In June, part of the Rev. Connell's parish was handed over to the new St. Benedict's, the second time the St Mark's parish had shrunk in 12 months.

It's unclear what exact church body the St Mark's association side originated from. It may have been the choir, from where many sports teams around this period were formed. Choir member Frederick Hopkinson, who would have taken part in the choral service that followed the Temperance Society conference on 20 November, was also the secretary of St Mark's Cricket Club. But it most likely sprang out of the Sunday school, as one of the "supplementary aids outside of school" designed to improve attendance.

St Mark's Sunday school was flourishing by 1880 and boasted 780 pupils a week. But encouraging pupils to remain at the school was a constant problem which led to a host of incentives, such as trips to the countryside and the handing out of attendance medals, to keep pupils attending. There is also a long tradition of football being used as an enticement. In June 1851, for instance, 3,000 scholars from six Manchester Wesleyan Methodist Sunday schools went on a day trip to the countryside, where "foot-balls, cricket, etc were provided for their amusements".

The formation of football clubs elsewhere also suggests a Sunday school link. Seven of the nine present-day major League clubs with church origins are now known to have originated from Sunday schools (Bolton, Fulham, QPR, Southampton and Tottenham had Church of England origins, Aston Villa was Wesleyan and Everton was Methodist). More specifically, they originated from their schools' Young Men's Bible Class, which typically consisted of men in their late teens and early 20s. The average age of St Mark's football team that first game was 19, representing precisely the age group the Anglican church had admitted it was struggling to retain. According to Paul Toovey's *Birth of the Blues*, nine of the 12 players that played in St Mark's first football match had in 1879 appeared for a St Mark's side called the Juniors – a popular name for Sunday school clubs. It also seems significant that none of them played for the Juniors side in 1880, suggesting they had progressed from a junior class to the young men's.

Of course, it's also possible the club simply started out with a group of young men having a kick-about in their spare time, and was later incorporated into the church's activities. They may have been introduced to the game by watching the association matches at the nearby Longsight Cricket Club during 1878. The St Mark's captain William Sumner, who had recently moved to the area, may also have provided the catalyst. The launch of the Lancashire FA Challenge Cup during the 1879-80 season would certainly have provided further inspiration to start playing the game. The competition was widely covered in the Manchester press and details of its trophy, unveiled in the spring of 1880, were stunning. Costing around £160, the 3ft 4in tall trophy was made of solid silver – adding glamour to a sport that had hitherto escaped the attention of the young men of West Gorton.

It may also be significant that in the same month that St Mark's football club was created, Banbridge Academy – where Connell once gave lectures – became one of four founding clubs of the Irish Football Association. Indeed, if Connell was still in contact with the Academy, events there might have influenced his decision to create a football club in his parish. It is also noticeable that wherever Connell went, sports clubs sprang up and flourished. In 1858 he delivered a lecture at Banbridge Young Men's Mutual Improvement Society, County Down entitled "The mental and moral improvement of young men". That year the Banbridge Cricket Club was created, one of the first examples of the sport being played in Northern Ireland. Harrogate also became a hotbed of cricket and rugby during Connell's time there, while a cricket club was created at St Mark's in the first summer he was appointed rector.

Men with a Mission

Although no firm evidence connects Connell to the creation of sports clubs in Northern Ireland and Harrogate, evangelicalism and "Muscular" Christianity were inextricably linked during this period. In Demember 1884 William Warburton, the president of the Manchester branch of the Society for Promoting Christianity among the Jews (whose cause Connell had championed in Harrogate) wrote a letter to the *Manchester Courier* urging Lancashire's foremost clubs to arrange fixtures in regions "where the mysteries of the dribbling code are yet unknown", and in particular, north Manchester. A former national treasurer of the Society was Lord Kinnaird, whose son later became president of the Football Association, while its president was Lord Shaftesbury, the greatest social reformer of his day. Shaftesbury was the main driving force behind the expansion of compulsory education and the shortening of the working week, reforms that were crucial to the spread of organised sport.

Shaftesbury was also president of the British Temperance League, which held a conference at Manchester's Free Trade Hall in November 1874. A conversation between chairman T B Smithies and Manchester missionary Jeremiah Chadwick illustrated the sense of urgency in the evangelical movement. "What kind of men have you got in Manchester? Are you improving or going backward", asked Smithies, to which

Chadwick replied: "I'm afraid we are getting worse".

Chadwick was a key figure in the Manchester offshoot of the London City Mission, another organisation over which Shaftesbury presided. Over the next few years Chadwick led a City Mission campaign to take the gospel of temperance to the railway and iron workers of East Manchester. Supported by senior figures in the railway industry, such as MSLR chairman Edward Watkin and L&Y director George Wilson, mass temperance meetings of up to 1,000 employees were held in railway's iron works at Newton Heath L&Y, Ashbury's and Gorton Tank.

Perhaps significantly, football and cricket teams sprang up in all three of these works around the time of the mass meetings. Reports of a Ashbury's works cricket team first appear a year after 1,000 employees attended a City Mission meeting there in January 1878, while the MSLR's Gorton Tank created an association team around the time of a City Mission mass meeting at the works in October 1883 (which was also attended Warburton). And in March 1878 – the year that the L&YR carriage works in Newton Heath created a cricket and football club – 500 of the works' employees attended an address by Bishop Fraser, organised by the Mission.

The subject of his address was temperance, a movement that saw "Muscular" Christianity as one of its main tools. At this time temperance campaigners believed that improved physical fitness led to lower alcohol consumption. At the Church of England's Temperance Society conference on 20 November 1880 the Rev. W M Johnson declared that "much of the drinking of the time had been brought on by the weakness of the frame. If all men were in good health there would be less drinking" (though one wonders whether a trip through time to witness post-match celebrations by Arsenal's footballers during the 1990s would have prompted him to alter his views).

Arthur Connell also attended the 20 November conference, and as chairman of the monthly Band of Hope temperance meeting at St Mark's, would be in little doubt that increased physical fitness was the primary antidote to alcoholic abuse, and the route to prosperity and salvation. Indeed, this earnest evangelicalism appears to be the most prominent strand of the early DNA of Manchester football. And although evidence is incomplete, this may be the best clue as to why, in the space of just two weeks in November 1880, the number of Manchester association clubs had jumped from one to five.

Young Man, there's a Place You Can Go

There was one other body that the ubiquitous Lord Shaftesbury presided over: the Young Men's Christian Association. The most successful evangelical organisation of the Victorian age, its principal aim was to offer young men of all denominations a religious-based alternative to the public house. By the 1870s it had discovered "the absurdity of attempting to gather together young men and women by forcing down their throats mere abstract theology of a more or less insipid nature". According to the *Courier*, in May 1876, this "solemn dullness", which might drive away "young men full of animal spirits" had been replaced by a "practical Christianity", one that "has to a certain extent to adapt itself to humanity".

The YMCA's many classes already allowed young men to learn book-keeping, shorthand and foreign languages, as well as improve their reading, writing, drawing, singing, arithmetic and speaking skills. Their minds could be further improved through the extensive reference library and reading rooms, as well as its chess clubs. But in October 1876 sport was incorporated into YMCA activities when it opened "one of the best, if not very best" gymnasiums in Manchester. "The great object of their institution was to promote Christianity among young men; but there was little objection to a little muscular Christianity", YMCA president Herbert Philips declared that month.

In June 1880 it announced the creation of a "large recreation ground where the young men can have facilities for healthy outdoor games, such as cricket, football, bowls, lawn tennis etc". The grounds would be on "five acres of Mr Carill-Worsley's land next to Platt Church in Rusholme", a site on which Manchester City FC's youth academy currently stands. A bicycle club was also created that month, rambling clubs were established and around 300 young Manchester men that year were given holidays at the YMCA's seaside home in Llandudno, Wales. All these attractions, plus the opportunity to dine at its city centre restaurant, were available for an annual fee of less than ten shillings, roughly half a week's wages. Not surprisingly, membership boomed. In 1878 they attracted 711 new members in Manchester, which grew to 990 new members in 1879 and 1,025 in 1880. Indeed, the need to compete with the YMCA's many attractions may have been one of the driving forces behind the creation of church football teams.

It's possible the YMCA played a role in the spread of the association game in Manchester. According to Bishop Fraser, 90% of the Manchester YMCA's members had moved to the city to work, and many would have arrived from hotbeds of football such as Birmingham and the Potteries, and in particular, the many footballing towns of Lancashire.

The Platt Lane sports fields were "easily accessible from the central buildings, as well as from the Alexandra and Longsight branches". Platt Lane, which became the home of Manchester Rangers rugby club, may have played a role in the creation of the Longsight Rangers rugby club. Its first recorded match, in October 1880, took place a month before St Mark's Rovers were created.

The New Idols

The Victorian men driving the YMCA's expansion into sport would probably be heartened that the five acres of land on Platt Lane are still used today to teach the values of self-discipline and hard work to young men. They would certainly be impressed by the scale of Manchester City FC's planned youth academy in Beswick, an 80-acre site that will contain 16 football pitches, a 7,000 capacity stadium and community facilities when it is completed in 2014.

On the edge of the Beswick academy site a new school, the Connell Sixth Form College, is due to open in September 2013. It is named after the family of Arthur Connell, though its pupils will receive a very different schooling than that of the Victorian children who attended Connell's St Mark's schools. In fact, the idea of mixed-sex classes, "theatre studies" and a religious studies course that invites pupils to "enjoy a really good discussion", with questions such as "does God exist?", would have appalled the puritanical Connell. As one anonymous letter-writer from Longsight told the *Courier* in October 1880, open debate was "regarded with pious horror" in church discussion groups.

Connell would certainly have little in common with the Chair of the founding governors of its school's board, a man who also serves as a director of the Catholic Trust, whose principal aim is "to promote the Catholic religion principally, but not exclusively, in England and Wales". But they would at least agree on the importance of education. By June 1881 St Mark's school had become one of the largest in Manchester, one of Connell's many achievements during his time in West Gorton. Community organisations also thrived during his tenure, as did the church's "Penny bank", a savings bank for low-income families. But maybe his greatest lasting achievement was helping establish football in the city.

And that throws up something of an irony.

According to David Bebbington's *Evangelicalism in Modern Britain*, church attendances began to decline in the 1870s, ushering in the so-called "Victorian crisis of faith". The extent of the problem was revealed by Bishop Fraser in his 6 November speech. A door-to-door survey of three Manchester parishes found that 49% of families had no religious affiliation, and in one parish only 27% of families belonged to a religious body.

In 1880 the Church's rallying call was "We must win the people", and the creation of football clubs was an important tool to further that goal. According to historian Keith Sandiford, almost a quarter of urban association clubs in Lancashire were formed by the clergy. By the early 1880s Blackburn and Preston, where church attendances were especially low, had become the new footballing hotbeds. The clergy's promotion of football appears to have helped stem the tide of young men leaving the Church. In 1882 Bishop Fraser confirmed 115 females and 87 males from four Manchester districts at a service at Prestwich parish church, a marked contrast to the female/male ratio of 5:1 recorded for the previous decade.

However, the game appeared to be acquiring its own religious characteristics. Following Blackburn Olympic's historic FA Cup victory in 1883, which made them the first working-men's team to win the trophy, the *Preston Chronicle* remarked on the "new idolatry" the sport had created.

> "We can put up with football, when played
> carefully; but, however carefully managed, we don't
> care for it when it becomes a sort of god, or all-
> absorbing worship, as it seems to be at Blackburn.
> The religion of many Blackburnians appears to be
> Football, and certain of the newspapers encourage
> this new idolatry amongst them."

In their evangelical drive to use team sport to promote Christianity, clergymen such as Arthur Connell may have inadvertently helped create its greatest competitor.

⁂

Hellenic Olympians had extraordinary minds. Blackburnian Olympians have remarkable feet. The other day the Association Challenge Cup was won by the Blackburn Olympic Football Club; and they went wild with delight about it at Blackburn. Somehow, in these latter days, many of the young people of Blackburn and thereabout, have been in a complete craze as to football. It has been their alpha and omega. How their minds are being improved we know not; but their feet are clearly in a highly-trained condition. Perhaps, they look upon this as an improvement of their *understandings*. We can put up with football, when played carefully; but, however carefully managed, we don't care for it when it becomes a sort of god, or all-absorbing worship, as it seems to be at Blackburn. The religion of many Blackburnians appears to be Football, and certain of the newspapers encourage this new idolatry amongst them. A few days ago one of the local journals devoted nearly six columns to football and footballers! How valuable the space of such a paper must be when it can set apart nearly an entire page to the ways and works of Blackburn footballers.

⁂

The Preston Chronicle on Blackburn's new-found "religion"

Gorton cricket clubs (1860-1873)

1st recorded appearance	Name	Possible origin
Jul 21 1860	Gorton	
May 27 1865	Gorton Works	Beyer Peacock foundry
Jun 25 1867	St Mark's (West Gorton)	
May 1869	West Gorton Perseverance	Temperance or Friendly Society
Jul 6 1869	West Gorton Star	
Jul 6 1869	West Gorton Albion	
Jul 13 1869	Gorton Schools	School
Aug 11 1869	Gorton United	
Aug 11 1869	Gorton Albert	
Jul 17 1871	West Gorton Claredon	
Aug 28 1871	West Gorton & District	
Jun 24 1872	West Gorton True Blues	Conservative or Orange Order
Jun 24 1872	West Gorton Union (2nd XI)	Union chapel or Union Iron works
Jul 1 1872	St Mark's Sunday School	C of E Sunday School
1873	Gorton National	School

Gorton sports clubs 1874-1879

Sport	First appearance	Name	Origin
Cricket	Aug 1874	Gorton True Blue	Conservative or Orange Order
Cricket	2 Aug 1874	Gorton-street Perseverance	Temperance or friendly society
Cricket	1874	West Gorton Union	Union chapel or Iron works
Cricket	2 Aug 1876	St Mark's Juniors	C of E Sunday School
Cricket	1876	Gorton-street True Blues	Conservative or Orange Order
Hare & hounds	12 Feb 1877	West Gorton Albion	
Cricket	1877	West Gorton Rangers	
Cricket	1877	West Gorton True Blue	Conservative or Orange Order
Cricket	26 Jun 1877	West Gorton Union Sunday School (2nd eleven)	Baptist Sunday School
Rugby	31 Dec 1877	Gorton Excelsior	
Rugby	31 Dec 1877	West Gorton	
Rugby	31 Dec 1877	Gorton Hornets	

Gorton sports clubs 1878-1881

Sport	First appearance	Name	Origin
Rugby	Jan 1880	Gorton Onward	Salvation Army
Cricket	1880	Gorton Juniors	Sunday School
Cricket	1880	Gorton Baptists	Union Baptist chapel
Cricket	19 Jul 1880	West Gorton Baptists	Union Baptist chapel
Rugby	11 Oct 1880	Longsight Rangers	Poss. Army Volunteers or YMCA
Rugby	6 Nov 1880	St Mark's Rovers	C of E
Football	13 Nov 1880	St Mark's	C of E
Rugby	3 Oct 1881	Longsight Rovers	
Cricket	Jun 1881	Clowes-st United	
Cricket	1881	Belle Vue Rovers	

1880 survey of three Manchester parishes

Denomination	Parish 1	Parish 2	Parish 3	Total	Total (%)
Anglican	88 (7.1%)	434 (24.1%)	261 (15.2%)	783	**16.5%**
Roman Catholic	94 (7.6%)	270 (15%)	620 (36.1%)	984	**20.1 %**
Non-conformist (see note 1)	147 (11.9%)	372 (20.6%)	105 (6.1%)	625	**13.1%**
Mormon	1				
Atheist	1				
"No pretense to Christian belief"			25 (1.5%)		
No place of worship / No or merest attachment	903 (73%)	727 (40.3%)	707 (41.1%)	2,337	**49.1%**
Total households	1,233	1,803 (out of 1,987)	1,719	4,755	

(Note 1) Breakdown of non-conformist affiliation from Parish 1: Wesleyan 53, Primitive Methodist 37, Independent 17, Baptist 16, Presbyterian 14, New Methodist Connection 8, Unitarian 1

CHAPTER 4

A MAN'S GAME

A month before the formation of St Mark's football club the area of West Gorton – and indeed the whole of Manchester – was scandalised by a court case involving sexual acts unheard of by the vast majority.

At 1am on Saturday 25 September a police raid on a fancy dress ball at the Temperance Hall on York Street, Hulme resulted in the arrest of 47 men. Some of the participants of the all-male gathering were dressed as historical figures such as Henry VIII, Richard III and Sir Walter Raleigh. But 22 of them were dressed as women, wearing gowns, "jewellery of a tawdry description" and make-up that "was in some cases an excellent imitation of the original". And in a further assault on Victorian sensibilities, under their gowns all but two of them were "fully got up as female".

Not surprisingly, the *Courier* reported that "the greatest interest was manifested in the case". Packed courtrooms heard the prosecutor describe the event as "one of the foulest and most disgraceful orgies that ever disgraced any town". According to the testimony of police officers, who had observed events from a nearby rooftop, men dressed as women had performed a series of dances including the "can-can" (which was played by a blind musician) and engaged in "indecent practices".

All 47 men were charged with inciting and soliciting each other "to commit improper actions", an offence that carried up to ten years imprisonment. A similar case in Liverpool had resulted in a sentence of four years hard labour and remarks by Manchester magistrate Richards, who complained in court about having "to sit and listen to this filth and obscenity", suggested similar sentences were likely.

However, possibly as a result of inconclusive police evidence, all 47 men were sentenced to be bound over for 12 months and ordered to pay a £50 bond. This was the equivalent of 6-12 months wages for a typical working man and resulted in ten of them being jailed for three months for non-payment.

The late Victorian age was one of rigidly defined gender roles and extremely limited access to material of a sexual nature, so this court case would have sent shock-waves through Manchester's communities. Sheffield, where nine of the defendants lived, was equally scandalised. The *Sheffield Daily Telegraph* even declared that

> "A considerable portion of the evidence was of a nature not only unfit for publication, but too bad ever to be indicated in general terms."

The sensationalist tabloid *Illustrated Police News* splashed the story over its front page while Manchester's newspapers, employing tactics that a modern-day Sunday tabloid would be familiar with, published the names and addresses of all 47 defendants.

Most readers would have been especially shocked by the appearance on the list of 30-year-old school master George Broughton, who was dressed as a woman that night. He lived with another of the defendants, 25-year-old draper John Cartwright, in Stalybridge. For the residents of West Gorton another named-defendant, Arthur Shawcross, would have been the focus of their attention. The unmarried 48-year-old mechanic lived just 100 yards from St Mark's church, at 11, Elizabeth Street. Living directly opposite was 51-year-old calico printer, Thomas Chew, whose sons – William, 18, and Walter, 15 – would soon play a crucial role in the development of football in Gorton.

Of the 18 men publicly named as being dressed as women, six were 21-years-old or younger, while one was just 16. One defendant claimed in court that Shawcross had introduced him to the event, so concerns about whether the 48-year-old had been in contact with the young men of the area would have been foremost on the minds of many residents. It's also possible that a "moral panic" spread throughout the community. The census

MEN DRESSED AS WOMEN! The front page of the populist Police News on 9 October, with illustrations of the police raid

EXTRAORDINARY OCCURRENCE IN MANCHESTER.

A FANCY BALL INTERRUPTED BY THE POLICE.

At the Manchester City Police Court this morning, there were brought before Messrs. Rickards, Railton, Kennedy, Bannerman, Goldschmidt, and Hardwicke, 47 men, on a charge of having, last night, assembled in a room off York-street, Hulme, for an unlawful and improper purpose. The gathering had partaken of the nature of a fancy-dress ball, and additional interest was caused by the appearance of eight of the defendants in female attire. The great majority of the men were in fancy costume, and the "make-up" of the *quasi* women was in some cases an excellent imitation of the original. Many of the defendants had, however, when captured, hastily divested themselves of their gaudy costumes, and now appeared thinly clad in skirts and bodices, with an occasional shawl wrapped around the wearer's head and shoulders. Some costumes were of the "Troubadour" type, two men in particular figuring very prominently in "trunk-hose and slashed doublet," with the usual three-cornered cloak appended to their backs. Intelligence of the "raid" had spread with great rapidity through the town, and the court was crowded to excess before the defendants arrived from the police cells at the Town Hall. The authorities, however, desirous of avoiding a scene, quietly transferred their prisoners to another court, where the proceedings were conducted in the presence of very few people.

Detective Caminada wished the prisoners to be remanded until Thursday next, when Mr. Cobbett would appear on behalf of the police to prosecute.

The prisoners were then remanded until Thursday next, and they were informed that bail would be accepted.

The first report of the fancy dress ball from the front page of the Manchester Courier, 27 September 1880 reveals that Shawcross had moved to Bell Street in Openshaw a year later, suggesting that it had become problematical for him to remain in West Gorton.

And quite how the Rev. Connell took the news one can only imagine, particularly as 1880 had already been an unfortunate year for him. As well as having to again deal with shrinking parish boundaries (and the reduced income that entailed), in April William Gladstone – whom Connell once angrily claimed had "robbed" the Church of Ireland of a vast land-holding – had become Prime Minister again. So news that a resident living close to the church had been cavorting with young men who were dressed in women's frocks and knickers may have sent the puritanical Connell into something approaching apoplexy.

The subject of masculinity was one that preoccupied the Church during this period, particularly its sizeable and vociferous evangelical arm. Clergyman and writer Charles Kingsley, a pioneer of "Muscular" Christianity, viewed manliness as an "antidote to the poison of effeminacy" that was "sapping the vitality" of the Church. In April 1880 Bishop Fraser admitted that he had previously been "somewhat prejudiced" against the YMCA, "for he thought there was something like an effeminate Christianity among the members". Declaring that the YMCA was indeed sufficiently masculine, Fraser reminded them that "nothing but a manly type of Christianity" would save young men from "the temptations of city life in Manchester". According to John Shelton Reed's *The Glorious Battle: The Cultural Politics of Victorian Anglo-Catholicism*, opposition to the ritualistic practises of some Anglican clergymen partly stemmed from the belief that they were "effeminate". Connell, a strong opponent of ritualism, would certainly have been horrified by the displays of effeminacy at the ball. And as an active campaigner against alcohol he would also have been outraged that these acts were carried out in his beloved Temperance Hall.

While we cannot know whether the scandal was a factor in the creation of the two St Mark's sports clubs a month later, "Muscular" Christians certainly believed that football represented the antithesis of homosexuality. According to

Richard Holt's *Sport and the British*, "at precisely the moment when the new norms of maleness were coming into force, the incarnation of the opposite of 'manliness' was defined in the form of homosexuality, which for the first time was generally designated a crime in 1885".

Manchester mayor John Bennett referred to the "manly" nature of sport three times during his key 1864 speech following the inaugural Manchester Athletic Festival. Three years earlier Rugby School headmaster Dr Temple explained how "shinning" (kicking an opponent below the knee) was encouraged in order to give his pupils "backbone". Although shinning had been banned by 1880, football remained a tough game and the dangers it posed became the subject of much debate. By 1884 violence during matches had reached dangerous and, in some cases fatal, levels. On 22 March that year a player died as a result of injuries he received during a game at Queen's Road, West Gorton.

According to the *Manchester Courier*, 24-year-old William Lennon "was dribbling the ball along the field, when he was charged by one of the opposite side, a youth named Manning". Lennon immediately "complained of feeling great pain in his abdomen" and left the game. He died three days later in Manchester Infirmary, the result of a ruptured bowel. The practice of "charging" was already a controversial one which, according to the *Gorton Reporter*, "frequently resulted in fatal accidents". A report on Lennon's death noted that

> "The dangers of football have this year been made
> more evident than ever. Scarcely a week has passed
> but there has been an accident, several of which
> have terminated fatally".

At the player's inquest "the jury were so impressed with the danger attended on 'charging' which the Association rules permit, that they recorded their recommendation that the rule be abolished". The only recorded match at Queen's Road that day was West Gorton's 7-0 defeat of newly-created Gorton Villa. As no other clubs are known to have existed in the area during this period, we can be fairly confident this was the match in question.

FATAL FOOTBALL ACCIDENT.

An inquest was held this morning by the deputy city coroner, Mr. S. Smelt, on the body of William Henry Lennon, aged 24, a slotter, lately residing at 59, Back-street, West Gorton. The evidence showed that on Saturday afternoon last the deceased, in company with a number of other young men, was playing football in a field off Queen's Road. He was dribbling the ball along the field, when he was charged by one of the opposite side, a youth named Manning. Both players fell to the ground, and when the deceased got up he complained of feeling great pain in his abdomen. He stopped playing and shortly afterwards went home. His mother noticed that he seemed to be in great pain, and asked what was the matter with him. He replied that he had been injured whilst playing football, and that he was suffering very much. She at once had him conveyed to the infirmary where he remained until his death, which occurred shortly before eight o'clock last night. He told his mother that the game was played fairly, and that it was quite by accident that he had been hurt.—Mr. B. Pollard, resident medical officer at the Manchester Infirmary, said he attended deceased during his illness, and since his death he had made a post-mortem examination. He found that the bowels had been ruptured and that the cause of death was peritonitis, brought on by the rupture.—At the close of the inquiry a considerable amount of discussion took place between the jurymen, a number of whom appeared to be in favour of adopting a recommendation to the effect that the rules which allowed charging in the game of football ought to be altered.—Mr. Smelt, however, pointed out that there was no one to whom he could forward such a recommendation, and ultimately a verdict of accidental death was returned.

The Manchester Courier's account of the fatal game

West Gorton contained remnants of the old St Mark's club, which had folded early in 1883 after losing several regular players. Most of the departing players are not recorded playing any football in the 1883-84 season, and the death of William Lennon may be an important clue as to why they had abandoned the sport.

Posh Kids FC

St Mark's first match, against Baptist of Macclesfield on 13 November 1880, appears to have taken place in an area known as Jennison's field, on the northern boundary of the Belle Vue pleasure gardens and close to its Hyde Road entrance. The game was probably played under Football Association rules, which had by now been amalgamated with the Sheffield Rules.

Some aspects of the game would have been virtually unrecognisable from modern-day football. The pitch had no touchlines (the only stipulation was a maximum size of 200y by 100y), four corner flags marked out the boundaries and tape was attached to the goals to form a crossbar of unknown height. Each team also had 12 men that day, which was allowable under association rules. Scrimmages – similar to a rugby scrum – were a common aspect of the game. One lasted over five minutes and towards the end of the match "scrimmages became the order of the day". The practice of "charging", which killed William Lennon nearly four years later, also featured. According to a match report, St Mark's player Heggs made an "excellent run up the side, passing four of the Baptist men in succession. Just after he was going to deliver the ball he was charged, and the ball taken from him".

But in others ways the game was similar to the one played today. Recent rule changes had introduced corners and goal kicks, and a new playing formation had just become established. According to football pioneer J J Bentley, writing in 1905, "about 1880 the three half-back system was generally adopted, and remains today." This new 2-3-5 "combination" formation was a passing game that marked the birth of the modern football – and St Mark's are the first recorded Manchester side to have played it. The city's first club, Manchester Association, played a 2-2-6 formation, an earlier variation of the passing game that probably originated in Scotland and was pioneered in England by the Royal Engineers. The 2-3-5 formation contained two full-backs, who played in a similar position to a modern-day centre-half. And as the five forwards often included two men on each wing, the formation does not seem too dissimilar to a modern-day 4-3-3 with attacking full-backs.

The St Mark's players appear to have been a close-knit group. Six of them lived close to the church (four on Clowes Street and two on adjoining Elizabeth Street), and most of them had played together for St Mark's Juniors cricket side in the summers of 1878 and 1879. The bulk of the football team, which consisted of six clerks, one student, the son of a local councillor and the son of a provision dealer, also shared a social status uncommon in Gorton. In fact, for an area so dominated by heavy industry, the team might even be characterised as "Posh Kids FC".

Their early matches showed no sign of the violence that later marred the game (though it should be noted that the match which caused Lennon's death in 1884 was described as a "pleasant" game by one newspaper report). The 4-0 defeat in the return match against Baptist on 22 January 1881 was called a "pleasant though rather one sided game" while the 5-0 defeat at Stalybridge on 12 March was described as "very friendly". That defeat meant the St Mark's record for the season was a dismal P8 W0 D3 L5 F2 A22. Although a win in the final game against an under-strength Stalybridge salvaged some pride, the season had been an unsuccessful one.

Its low point was a 7-0 defeat at home to Hurst, a bruising encounter in which the "very sloppy state" of the ground caused "very numerous" falls. A match report described the Hurst forwards as "working together like machinery" that day, something to which the young St Mark's men no doubt aspired. Indeed, the need to be more machine-like might explain an influx of new players from manual occupations during the 1881-82 season, including 18-year-old machine works apprentice John Bottomley and 24-year-old clog maker Joseph Clegg, who played in the opening match on 15 October 1881. By 3 December three more manual labourers had joined the club: 23-year-old boiler maker James McKenna, a player named Taylor –

likely to be 23-year-old carriage maker James Taylor or unemployed wagon maker Samuel Taylor – and a player named Roberts, who was either 19-year-old labourer James Roberts or his 17-year-old brother Charles, a fitter in an engineering works.

Manchester football was still firmly in the shadow of rugby throughout the 1881-82 season. Indeed, on 30 January 1882 six of the 15 England players selected for a rugby match against Ireland were from Manchester clubs. But the association game was gradually gaining ground. On 4 March the winning St Mark's goal in the 2-1 defeat of Newton Heath was celebrated "amidst loud cheers" from the Longsight crowd, suggesting a large attendance. St Mark's finished the season with a respectable record of P12 W5 D1 L6 F18 A22 and, with football now the country's fastest-growing sport, had every reason for optimism.

However, the next season would be their last.

The Blackburn "Roughs"

Around this time religious bodies lost control of many of the sports teams they had founded, including the Christ Church Sunday school side in Bolton, which cut its ties with the Anglican church in 1877 and re-formed as Bolton Wanderers. Football's split from its Church origins meant it was also separated from the Church's view of how and why the game should be played. Supporters of "Muscular" Christianity believed that sport existed in order to create good moral character in young men so they could be moulded into Christian gentlemen. And central to this idea was the belief that "fair play" was more important than winning. It was an ethos that had its roots in the Manchester Mechanics Institute Christmas parties of the 1850s – where football was accompanied by a "dance around the May pole, leap frog, running in sacks" and a jousting tournament – and the Sunday school outing, where football was followed by a picnic and other games.

But for the young men of Manchester, the heroics of Lancashire mill town football would have been the stuff of dreams. In March 1881 Darwen became the first working-class side to reach the FA Cup semi-finals, following their 15-0 defeat of Romford. A year later Blackburn Rovers were the first to reach the final, where they lost to the most aristocratic of England's football clubs, the Old Etonians. Rovers's cup-run appears to have had a significant impact on Manchester football. The two Manchester association clubs that were formed in the weeks before the final were both named "Rovers", while recently-formed Haughton Dale also began using the name.

The FA Cup was finally lifted by Northern working-men in March 1883, when Blackburn Olympic beat Old Etonians 2-1. According to Richard Sander's *Beastly Fury*, Olympic were a

> "solidly working-class side which included four cotton workers, a plumber and an iron worker and whose home was a "sloping mud-bath of a pitch behind the Hole i' th' Wall pub – so called because bootleg liquor used literally to be sold through a hole in the wall".

This strand of football possessed a spirit much closer to the rough-and-tumble of medieval football than the public school game. A match between Blackburn Rovers and Stoke in December 1879 ended after 10 minutes when Rovers left the pitch following a disputed goal. The following November a game between Rovers and Darwen was abandoned after the 12,000-strong Blackburn crowd – dubbed "Blackburn roughs" by one commentator – repeatedly spilled onto the pitch. According to the ensuing FA enquiry the match even saw a Rovers player called Suter drop an opponent on his head in front of onrushing fans.

The changing character of the association game in Manchester is best illustrated by events at Belle Vue Rangers, whose first documented appearance was in January 1882. Their home matches appear to have been played on common land off Queen's Road, also known as Clemington Park, just across the road from the St Mark's ground. Both clubs were close to the eastern entrance of Belle Vue pleasure gardens, which attracted around two million visitors a year. Those visitors were not noted for their sobriety. Indeed, in 1880 the easy availability of alcohol in and around the gardens prompted a letter to the *Courier* complaining about their drunken behaviour on Saturdays. So it's likely that games were played to a rowdy backdrop. And the presence of women spectators, which appears to have been a common feature of football matches in this period, would hardly dampen the boisterousness. As a letter-writer to *Courier* noted in January 1880, "these unseemly exhibitions of brute force are received by the ladies with approval". As the size of football crowds throughout Manchester grew so did their influence, including the baiting of players and stoking of controversy. By April 1884 the issue of Manchester's "rough" football fans was one of particular concern to the *Courier's* football correspondent, "Veteran". As well as the mobbing of referees, and "stoning and otherwise maltreating players", "Veteran" was particularly scornful of fans who excitedly yelled out "that the absolute annihilation of the whole opposing team would cause no actually poignant grief to him".

Belle Vue Rangers's 5-4 defeat away to Endon Reserves on 4 November 1882 was described as a "very unpleasant game" in which Belle Vue were forced to play against the wind for 75 minutes after Endon refused to change ends at half time. According to a match report "both of the umpires' watches were found to be stopped when time should have been called".

For football's authorities, the new breed of footballer was a problem that had to be dealt with. For the young working men of Manchester they were the new role models, ones who placed glory above moral improvement.

The End of St Mark's

The St Mark's side was probably restricted to parishioners, as was common practice for Anglican church teams during this period. However, finding eleven church-going young men to represent them proved to be a problem in the 1882-83 season. They were a man short for a game on 28 October, and on 4 November could only muster eight players for the game at Hurst Clarence. On 2 December they only fielded ten men for an away game at Marple. William Sumner, an engineering student who had captained St Mark's since their formation, was injured after suffering a "nasty fall" early in the game – the second serious injury recorded to a player in a St Mark's match in just over nine months. There's no record of Sumner playing for the club again, and at this point the season goes rapidly downhill. On 6 January they lost 4-2 to Marple at Belle Vue, a side they had drawn away to a month earlier with only nine fit men. The season's record now stood at P7 W0 D3 L4 F5 A16.

On 13 January St Mark's were scheduled to play Manchester Association at Greenheys, but there is no record of the match being played. This was the second time in just over a month that a scheduled fixture was not recorded as taking place. The following week Belle Vue were the only local side recorded as playing. They were captained by Walter Chew, and included warehousemen Edward Groves, both of whom had played for St Mark's in their first game of the season. On 27 January they were joined by St Mark's veteran Edward Kitchen for Belle Vue's game at Macclesfield Wanderers. It was a bruising encounter. According to a match report, Macclesfield "played a rough game even charging their opponents when the ball was six yards over the goal line".

Belle Vue didn't play again for five weeks. The next recorded game featuring a Gorton club was on 3 February when St Mark's lost 2-0 away to Broadbottom. The ten-man side featured four Belle Vue players from the Macclesfield game (three of whom had previously played for St Mark's), two other St Mark's veteran players, and four new players. It was also the last time the name of St Mark's was recorded in a football match involving a Gorton side.

And at this point the picture becomes blurred. On 17 February a side called "West Gorton" lost 7-0 away to Bentfield. Walter Chew captained the nine-men side, which included his brother William and Edward Kitchen, a St Mark's veteran who had played for Belle Vue three weeks earlier. Curiously, there is no record of any of the remaining six players appearing for any other Gorton club. The following week the *Gorton Reporter* records that a side called "West Gorton Association" played recently-created opponents Middleton at Gorton. Also captained by Walter Chew , the nine-man side contained three players from the team that played in Bentfield a week earlier, two who had probably started the season for St Mark's, a Belle Vue player and two new faces.

St Mark's had been referred to by various names during the 1882-83 season. For instance, the *Courier* recorded the side as "St Mark's" for the match against Manchester Association on 25 November, while the *Manchester Guardian* listed them as "West Gorton". The club had also been referred to as "St Mark's, West Gorton", "St Mark's (Longsight)" and "West Gorton (St Mark's)", and the parentheses were probably used to avoid being confused with a more established association club called St Mark's in Blackburn. However, the appearance of the name "West Gorton Association" appears to mark a significant change.

During this period, match details published in newspapers were supplied by club secretaries, and the reason St Mark's had been listed under different names is because the details had been sent in by their opponents. But the match report for the 24 February game was published in the *Gorton Reporter*, which meant it would have been supplied by the West Gorton club. If this was the Church side it's unlikely that Arthur Connell would have allowed them to cast off the name of his parish, indicating that this was a different club.

West Gorton Association's formation date is unclear. A month earlier, on 6 January, a side called "West Gorton (a team)" are recorded as playing away to new club Greenheys. As St Mark's played at their Belle Vue ground that day, this may be West Gorton Association's first recorded game. The club probably played on land beside the Union Iron works, identified in the 1906 *Book of Football* as the first ground of a "West Gorton Association Football Club". This suggests that the club had iron works origins, particularly as a local called Gorton Tank Rovers (representing MSL Railway's "Gorton Tank" iron works) had played its first recorded match three months earlier. It's also possible that the clubs were already well-established by this point, but had only played internal or inter-works matches that were not recorded in newspapers.

Although evidence is incomplete, it appears that the St Mark's players in the 24 February line-up had joined – or possibly helped create – the new West Gorton club around the time their church team had folded. If so, religious demands made on players may have played a role in St Mark's demise. In 1887 members of an Anglican club in Southampton, St Mary's Young Men's Association, were told that they would have to take part in parochial work, such as Sunday school teaching, in order to remain in the side. That resulted in the players breaking away from their church origins shortly afterwards and eventually renaming themselves Southampton FC.

However, West Gorton Association's match on 24 February was also the club's last, most likely due to the increasing danger the game posed (which might also explain why Newton Heath's season ended early on 17 February). Indeed, during the 1882-83 season violence in both football codes had reached dangerous levels. Football was a very similar game to rugby during this period, and in October it was claimed that the "dribbling game" may even have been the more violent of the two codes. Listing the injuries that had occurred in association games in the Manchester area during one Saturday, the *Courier's* football correspondent noted that

"A collar bone was broken at one place, a jaw bone
and nose were, to quote the wording of the
announcement, "smashed" at another, whilst a
gashed face, requiring the immediate attention of a
surgeon, was all that resulted in the third."

The "smashed" jawbone and nose may have been related to the fact, revealed in the *Courier's* "Football Notes" a month earlier, that head-butting an opponent in the face was permitted in matches.

On 8 January "Football Notes" read more like the in-patient records of a hospital casualty ward. During the city's biggest rugby match, played between Manchester FC and Marlborough Nomads in front of 15,000 spectators at Whalley Range, an unnamed Manchester player "deliberately seized a diminutive player of the opposite team, who had just wriggled his way through a scrummage, and after lifting him into the air, smashed him, with all his full force, full length to the ground". In a game played in Manchester the previous Monday the most gifted player on one team "was generally knocked into a jelly" and finished the match unconscious with a sprained ankle, twisted knee, wrenched shoulder, severely bruised arm and a bent nose. The paper also recorded injuries in the association game. A Darwen player was "seriously injured" after he was knocked unconscious by a kick to the ribs (labelled "charging"), the third serious injury to a Darwen player that season.

FOOTBALL NOTES.

"It is no secret that there is a widespread objection to the game, on account of the rough style in which it is often played, and on account of the occasional accidents which unfortunately result therefrom."

So we wrote last week, and we now propose showing in what respects there is room for improvement. One of the most fruitful sources of "accidents" in the football field, is the brutal way in which charging down is often done by what are playfully called "bull-dogs." The main efforts of these gentlemen are directed to disabling an opponent at every available opportunity, and the favourite method employed is to "butt" him violently with the head in the stomach, or, if possible, in the mouth. A well-directed effort of this nature seldom fails in its object, and it is no unfrequent spectacle to see, in the course of a game, numbers of disabled players writhing about in momentary agony. Any dentist of repute will tell you that he has numberless cases of football players who have to be supplied with odd front teeth at times. Now this practice is no less unnecessary than brutal. If an opponent will stand the full brunt of a charge, he will probably, in the shock itself, be quite enough punished

The Courier's condemnation of football violence from 1883

Concern over the changing nature of the game had been a newspaper theme since at least 1878. In March that year an association player had been acquitted of manslaughter following the death of an opponent, the *Grantham Journal* declared that

> "The old-fashioned and thoroughly English game
> has lost some of its real and genuine manliness in
> the attempt to give it new features and to subject it
> to new rules. It is true that in the old days players
> expected to have their shins barked, and to receive
> an ugly wound now and then, but there was no
> sham playing of the ball with the hand rather than
> the foot, no brutal 'charging' of adverse players, no
> violent grappling of an opponent under
> circumstances which make the grappling dangerous.
> The old game without the 'shinning' was one of
> which Englishmen may be justly proud. The new
> game is one that cannot be played without putting
> every parent in fear for the physical safety of his
> son."

Differing reasons were put forward to explain the increased violence in the game. For some of football's early pioneers the the introduction of profit into what was once a purely amateur pastime was the root cause. "(Nothing) would be sufficient to describe the atrocities you commit with your "gate money webs", wrote one contributor to *Football* in October 1882. Others blamed the influx of Scottish players into the English game. In September 1884 another adherent of amateurism claimed in *The Athlete* that the "employment of the scum of the Scottish villages has tended, in no small degree, to brutalise the game."

On 6 December 1882 the problem of violent play was debated at a meeting of the Football Association's National Conference held in Manchester. The Conference proposed changes to the

VOU0754305

Order by: 31/03/19
Min spend: £60
Max reward: £25

New customers only. One first shop voucher per customer and per registered address. Voucher cannot be used in conjunction with any other voucher offer. Delivery slots subject to availability and location. To check if Ocado delivers in your area, please visit **ocado.com/postcode**. Discount will only be applied to products in the following categories: Fresh, Food Cupboard, Bakery, Frozen, Soft Drinks, Tea & Coffee, Toiletries, Finger Foods, Baby Meals & Drinks and Baby Toiletries. Minimum spend excludes tobacco products, postage stamps, infant formula, the purchase of Ocado Gift Vouchers, and food donations with Ocado. Voucher minimum spend is specified in voucher details. Standard minimum spend £40 per order (excluding 20th-24th December). Statutory minimum alcohol pricing will apply. This voucher includes a free Annual Smart Pass: once activated, this includes free delivery for 12 months (excluding 20th-24th December). Deliveries limited to one per day. For full Terms & Conditions refer to Grocery Vouchers at **ocado.com/terms**.

VOU0754305

Order by: 31/03/19
Min spend: £60
Max reward: £25

New customers only. One first shop voucher per customer and per registered address. Voucher cannot be used in conjunction with any other voucher offer. Delivery slots subject to availability and location. To check if Ocado delivers in your area, please visit **ocado.com/postcode**. Discount will only be applied to products in the following categories: Fresh, Food Cupboard, Bakery, Frozen, Soft Drinks, Tea & Coffee, Toiletries, Finger Foods, Baby Meals & Drinks and Baby Toiletries. Minimum spend excludes tobacco products, postage stamps, infant formula, the purchase of Ocado Gift Vouchers, and food donations with Ocado. Voucher minimum spend is specified in voucher details. Standard minimum spend £40 per order (excluding 20th-24th December). Statutory minimum alcohol pricing will apply. This voucher includes a free Annual Smart Pass: once activated, es includes free delivery for 12 months (excluding 20th-24th December). everies limited to one per day. For full Terms & Conditions refer to Grocery Vouchers at **ocado.com/terms**.

30% off

your first grocery shop

+ FREE deliveries for a year

◎ ocado

30% off

your first grocery shop

+ FREE deliveries for a year

◎ ocado

sport's rules, which were published on 8 January 1883. Rule 10, which stated that "Neither tripping nor hacking shall be allowed, and no player shall use his hands to hold or push his adversary" now read (proposed changes in italics):

> "Neither tripping nor hacking, *nor jumping at a player*, shall be allowed, and no player shall use his hands to hold or push his adversary, *or charge him from behind.*"

Although going some way to curtail the violence, "charging" a player – the act that lead to the death of a Gorton player 15 months later – was still permitted, as was "jumping at a player" who was shielding the ball with his back to goal. And with referees' cautions not yet a part of the game and sendings-off only permitted for the possession of dangerous footwear, even the most violent breach of the rules would have resulted in little more than a free-kick to the opposition team. For the time being, Manchester's young footballers were being offered scant protection from brutal play.

The dangers posed by the game might explain why St Mark's struggled to find players. In a time before universal healthcare and benefits, a serious injury sustained in a football pitch could result in severe financial hardship. Indeed, West Gorton's game against Broadbottom on 17 February was played as a benefit for a Hurst player who had broken his leg. It's also worth noting that, in a sport increasingly dominated by young men employed in heavy manual labour, four of the five St Mark's regulars who deserted the game that season were clerks, while the other was the son of a flour dealer.

The 1882-83 season had offered great promise for Gorton's four association clubs. But at the end of one of the bloodiest seasons in football's history, Belle Vue Rangers were the only team left standing.

CHAPTER 5

THE CREATION OF GORTON ASSOCIATION

At the start of the 1883-84 season Manchester football barely registered on the national consciousness. The city hadn't entered a single club in the first round of the 1882-83 FA Challenge Cup, despite that fact that 19 of the 84 clubs in the competition were Lancastrian. The sometimes shambolic nature of Manchester football had been highlighted on 6 January 1883, when Newton Heath's home match with Manchester Association was cancelled because Newton Heath "could not furnish a ball". But nine months later an even bigger mystery arose when a football club in West Gorton disappeared.

Are You Belle Vue in Disguise?

On 6 October 1883 a side called West Gorton played Hurdsfield of Macclesfield. It was the first football match involving a Gorton club since March. But West Gorton's origins became the subject of a lengthy exchange in the *Courier's* sports pages, one which provides clues to the origins of Manchester City FC.

It began two days after the Hurdsfield match, when the *Courier's* football correspondent, "Dribbler", wrote

> "I am informed that Sumner who played for West
> Gorton last season, and which club has broken up,
> will play for Manchester Association next
> Saturday."

A week later West Gorton's Hon. Secretary, P Howarth, responded

"I noticed in your last issue a paragraph to the effect that the West Gorton Association F.C. was no more. Permit me to contradict that report as being untrue. Besides, such a statement tends to mislead clubs with whom we have engagements."

The following week "Dribbler" gave his reply.

"It appears I was right after all about the West Gorton club being abolished. The Belle Vue Rangers, the secretary of which wrote on the subject that the statement was misleading, have taken on the name of the deceased West Gorton, hence the misunderstanding."

This prompted the following angry response from Howarth.

WEST GORTON ASSOCIATION FOOTBALL CLUB.
To the Editor of the Manchester Courier.

Sir,—From what source "Dribbler" gets his information I can't tell, but it is "quite wrong." At the beginning of the present season several of the older members of the West Gorton club notified their intention of giving up the game, whilst others left the club to join another. The Belle Vue Rangers then cast off their name, and joined with the remaining members of the West Gorton club, thus keeping the club from breaking up, so that there is no hankering about it. With this I hope "Dribbler" will be satisfied.—Yours, &c.,   P. HOWARTH, Hon. Sec.
    201, Yew Tree-terrace, Gorton-lane, Gorton, Oct. 29.

However, the line-up for West Gorton's first game of the 1883-84 season, which contained nine Belle Vue players from the previous season and two unknowns, shows that this was merely

Belle Vue under a different name. Although three members of the side had previously played for St Mark's, they had been much more closely associated with Belle Vue, where they were regulars during the 1882-83 season.

The disagreement between "Dribbler" and Howarth may have been the result of a misunderstanding. "Dribbler" was clearly referring to the St Mark's club, which had also been called "West Gorton". But Howarth was probably referring to a new West Gorton club – one containing the remnants of St Mark's – that had limped on to the end of the season.

It's not clear why Belle Vue Rangers cast off its name at the start of the 1883-84 season. It was one of at least eleven Manchester sports clubs that were called "Rangers", and its prevalence suggests the name may have been linked to a city-wide organisation. The Volunteer movement, which actively promoted field sports during this period, is one likely candidate. Belle Vue was the home of the 7th Lancashire Artillery Volunteers, and the day before the football club was launched the annual prize-giving for the 2nd Manchester Rifle Volunteers was held there. Other possible places of origin are the YMCA in Longsight and the Belle Vue pleasure gardens, both of which were actively promoting sport during this period.

The change of name may have signalled the club's split from their roots. More likely it was to acquire West Gorton's superior fixture list. In the 1882-83 season two of Belle Vue's six recorded opponents were reserve sides, and none of the six opponents from that ill-tempered season appeared in the 1883-84 fixture list. As the sole football club in a district of 36,000 people, West Gorton were in a unique position to grow. An attendance of 1,000 was recorded for a home match in October, while a home match in February 1884 attracted 600. The following month a second club sprang up in the district. Called Gorton Villa, they might have originated from an area of the same name near Gorton Mill on the eastern side of the township, or may have named themselves after Aston Villa, who played in the quarter-finals of the FA Cup that month. It was the tenth new association club to be formed in the Manchester area that season, bringing the region's total to 29.

Manchester's Two FAs

By the start of the 1884-85 season Manchester football was challenging rugby as the city's main winter sport. Sadly, it was challenging little else. The city's sole representative in the FA Cup, Manchester Association, had been beaten 15-0 by Queen's Park of Glasgow in the second round the previous season. No Manchester club took part in the 1884-85 FA Cup, but in October eight of the area's clubs – Hurst Park Road, Heywood, Greenheys, Newton Heath, Eccles, Manchester AFC, Levenshulme and Hurst Clarence – took part in the first round of the Lancashire FA Cup. Seven of them lost, scoring just four goals between them and conceding 46. Only Newton Heath's 4-0 win over Haydock Temperance salvaged Manchester pride.

However, the game was at least growing in popularity. By September 1884 enough clubs existed to form the Manchester District Football Association. According to a 15 September 1884 report by the *Courier's* football correspondent, "Veteran"

> "The increase in the number of association clubs already noted is not the only indication that the 'dribbling' game is every year gaining additional ground and supporters. In the immediate neighbourhood, for instance, not only have new association candidates for public favour sprung up on all sides, but an effort, which bids fair to be successful, has been made to blend the local clubs into one harmonious whole."

But harmony was in short supply in the football world at this time. The Manchester FA was born in the middle of an intense power struggle between the London-based FA and Lancastrian clubs, one which threatened to split the game in two. In May and June 1884 the FA held meetings in London to tackle what it saw as the growing menace of professionalism, which resulted in Preston North End being thrown out of the FA Cup and the introduction of tough new rules that only allowed player payments to cover travel and hotel expenses and loss of pay.

However, by this time the weight of numbers favoured the Lancashire game. The Lancashire FA now had 104 member clubs, an increase of 20 from the 1882-83 season. Some of them decided to fight back, and chose Manchester as the focal point of the revolt. On 30 October the breakaway British Football Association was formed at a meeting of 37 clubs held at the Dog and Partridge Hotel in Manchester. The rebel clubs included Accrington, Bolton Wanderers, Burnley, Preston North End, Aston Villa and Sunderland. Representatives from Newton Heath and Hurst also attended the meeting that day, despite the two clubs being founding members of the Manchester FA.

Two years earlier another meeting in Manchester, held on 6 December 1882 between the English, Scottish, Welsh and Irish FAs, had sought to establish a common set of rules. That meeting led to the creation of the first international competition, the British Home Championship, in January 1884 as well as the formation of the International Football Association Board, a body that still regulates the laws of the game today.

The administration of football had become more formalised in the two years between these crucial meetings. Pitch markings were introduced for the first time in 1883, and may have been connected to another problem facing football's authorities: the behaviour of fans. On 8 April 1884 the *Manchester Courier's* football correspondent, "Veteran", declared that

> "Something must be done, moreover, to stamp out
> the rowdyism which of late has disgraced the
> playing of football, and notably of association
> football, in this part of the world."

The formation of the Manchester FA may have been part of an attempt to tackle the twin dangers of professionalism and "rowdysim". Certainly it was run by people actively involved in the "moral and mental improvement" of young men. The reigns of power were held by members of Manchester AFC, the city's oldest club. Manchester FA president, Mr W Colbert, was also president of Manchester AFC, and its hon. treasurer, Mr A R

Andrews, was a club member. And running Manchester AFC were men acting as the city's moral and social guardians. Its president, J C Stewart, was a former president of the Manchester YMCA and headmaster of the Boys Refuge Industrial School, while vice-president J R Lever and committee member W C Hardy were members of the Manchester Athenaeum.

The rules of the Manchester FA were adopted at the Grand Hotel, on Aytoun Street, where rugby was also governed. Members had to be "within a radius of eight miles from the Manchester Exchange" and a representative "each from the twelve first-named clubs" sat on its committee. Initially, membership consisted of 16 clubs: Manchester Association, Manchester Arcadians, Dalton Hall, Greenheys, Levenshulme, Hurst, Hurst Park Road, Hurst Brook Olympic, Hurst Clarence, Pendleton Olympic, Haughton Dale, West Gorton, Eccles, West Manchester, Thornham and Newton Heath LYR.

Soon they were joined by another side. On 25 October 1884 the *Gorton Reporter* revealed that a new club, called Gorton Association, had been formed. It was the city's 31st association club, and the fifth to be created in the Gorton area. And it was the one that would evolve into Manchester City Football Club.

Gorton Association's ground was to the south of Belle Vue pleasure gardens off Pink Bank Lane. Its exact location is unclear, but it may have been where the hockey pitches of the Manchester Regional Hockey Centre are now located, or the current site of St Peter's RC High School that lies directly opposite.

Captain Improbable and His Men

The first recorded match at Pink Bank Lane was on 8 November, when a Gorton 2nd XI defeated Eccles (2nd XI) 4-2. The following Saturday the first team played their first recorded game, a 4-1 victory at home to Gorton Villa. After a goalless draw at home to Heywood St James on 22 November, the team line-up was recorded for the first time and provides important clues about the club's characteristics. The team's captain is listed only by his surname of Turner. On 15 March 1884 a trial match for a Manchester v Liverpool district game had taken place between "The Probables" and "The Improbables". Appearing for the latter was a right winger called W Turner, a regular for Dalton Hall. His team-mate that day was Edward Groves, a star player for West Gorton and Belle Vue Rangers, who played for Gorton Association later that season. Turner played at No.7 for Dalton Hall – the exact position Gorton's captain played – indicating that this is probably the same player. It also means that Gorton's captain had no known ties to the area.

The first known line-up, on 15 November 1885, also provides important clues to the club's origins. Four of the side had played for West Gorton a month earlier, and three of those had been regulars for Belle Vue Rangers in the 1882-83 season. Only two had played regularly for St Mark's, while five had no known connection to any West Gorton club. By the end of the season, eight of the club's 28 first-team players had previously appeared for Belle Vue Rangers but only six had played for St Mark's.

And at this point it is important to address the issue of City's formation date, one that has been clouded by the early histories of the club.

The History of the History

Early History.

Unlike most of the clubs whose history we have already traced, Manchester City cannot claim to be one of the oldest clubs playing the game. In fact, the City F.C. was formed out of what was left of the old Ardwick Club. The latter organisation originated in the early eighties, when a number of young men formed a club. Amongst these were Mr. William Lee, who was secretary; Mr. W. L. Furniss, and Mr. W. Chew. These gentlemen started the Ardwick Club.

The earliest written history of City, from 1898

The first recorded account of the club's early days, a 950-word article in the *Golden Penny* magazine from December 1898, places Manchester City FC's formation to the "early eighties". As Furniss did not move to Gorton until at least November 1883, the article is clearly referring to the creation of Gorton AFC as City's starting point. In November 1900 the *Golden Penny* published another history of the club. In this version the club's formation was dated to "the eighties" rather than the "early eighties", and Lee, Furniss and Chew were called the "prime movers" in the club's creation.

But in 1906 an anonymously-written article in a monthly magazine, called the *Book of Football*, re-wrote City's history.

> "Like many famous organizations, Manchester City began in a small way. It came into existence in the year 1880, and the father of the club was Mr. W. Chew. It was originally called the West Gorton Association Football Club. The first field procured was situated just off Clowes Street – the site is now covered by Messrs. Brooks & Doxey's works. In the following season the club migrated to the present Kirkmanshulme Cricket Ground, but owing to the damage wrought to the cricket-pitch, the followers of the summer game were very irate, and West Gorton's sojourn there was a short one.
>
> When the club lost the use of the Kirkmanshulme Cricket Ground, they were temporarily without a home, and virtually the club was disbanded, but an effort was made to revive it, and in 1884 the club started again as the Gorton Association Football Club."

Although subsequent histories have assumed that this account referred to St Mark's as the founding club, the fact that St Mark's were never called "West Gorton Association", and that there is no record of them playing at the Brooks & Doxey site, suggests otherwise. The *Book of Football* is more likely to be referring to a separate club, one that was first recorded playing in 1883 and probably had iron works origins.

In 1930 the first detailed history of the club, Fred Johnson's 116-page *Manchester City: A Souvenir History*, also used 1880 as the starting point. This was the first history to mention St Mark's in connection to City.

> "The Manchester City Association Football Club cannot claim such an ancient lineage as some members of the League, but its origin is directly traceable to 1880. The club wound up its career after a short season at the Kirkmanshulme cricket ground. Prior to this, however, some other pioneer enthusiasts for the Association game had started the West Gorton club (colours scarlet and black) their ground being in Queen's Road, West Gorton, and several former St Mark's players joined. In season 1884-5 operations were resumed under the name Gorton AFC, and the ground was in Pink Bank Lane. Colours, black jersey and white cross".

As virtually all of the club's records had been lost in a fire at Hyde Road in 1920, it's likely that Johnson's formation date was taken directly from the *Book of Football*. All subsequent histories have used the 1880 starting date, including Andrew Ward's 1984 book, *The Manchester City Story*, which was the first to state categorically that St Mark's was the founding club. Its findings were based on an unpublished book written by City fan Tony Heap in the 1970s.

However, Gorton AFC's first recorded line-up in November 1884 (see page 101) sheds the most light on the club's origins. At least five of the side had previously played for Belle Vue, while only three had played for St Mark's. Some of the players had also played for West Gorton a month earlier, while four had no known connection to any of the clubs in West Gorton club. Other evidence clearly shows that Gorton AFC was not merely St Mark's re-formed. St Mark's was a church team made up exclusively of Anglican parishioners. In contrast, Gorton AFC had no official ties to the Anglican Church, and the fact it was funded by a Liberal Unitarian means it would have been open to players of other denominations. Furthermore, two of the three players with known ties to St Mark's football club – Kitchen and Hopkinson – had been out of the game for 20 months while the third, Walter Chew, was much more closely identified with Belle Vue Rangers. Indeed, Walter Chew's first appearance for Belle Vue, on 14 January 1882, took place on the same day his elder brother William played for St Mark's. It's also significant that none of St Mark's opponents from the 1882-83 season appear on Gorton's 1884-85 fixture list. The new club also played under the jurisdiction of the Football Association, which St Mark's did not, and lastly, its name represented the whole Gorton area, not just West Gorton. Indeed, according to the census rolls, only six of the players from Gorton AFC's first recorded line-up lived in West Gorton.

St Mark's certainly played an important role in laying the groundwork for Gorton AFC's creation, as did Belle Vue Rangers and West Gorton Association, but the foundations of Manchester City FC were not laid until October 1884.

Gorton Association, not St Mark's, is the club that would evolve into Manchester City.

However, early histories should never be disregarded lightly. So before moving on, a closer examination of their texts is required. And perhaps not surprisingly, given the complexities of practically everything else connected to City's early history, a peeling away of the surface layer reveals yet more intrigue, scandal and personality clashes.

The *Golden Penny* was owned by Manchester publishing magnate Edward Hulton jnr, who became City's chairman in 1902. In 1904 Hulton unveiled plans to relocate to a new 60,000-capacity stadium, a move that would have resulted in him taking complete control of the club. However, after the plan was vetoed by the brewing interests on the City board, Hulton walked away from the club. In 1905 John Allison – a close ally of Hulton – became City's chairman, a position he held when the *Book of Football* (published by Hulton's friend Alfred Harmsworth, who owned the *Daily Mail*) came out.

The battle over the new stadium was referred to in the *Book of Football*, which stated that "some selfish people have stood in the way" of the club moving to a new ground. This suggests that Allison, the last remaining Hulton ally on the board, played a role in the writing of the article, and may even have been its sole author. Allison's fingerprints can also be found on the 1900 *Golden Penny* history. Although largely a re-write of the 1898 article, the claim that City "certainly owe a great debt of gratitude" to Allison, plus a sentence promoting Allison's hydropathic baths in Ardwick, had been mysteriously inserted.

But Allison did not become involved with the club until the 1889-90 season, which might explain why the *Book of Football* incorrectly dates the move to Hyde Road as 1889. Although Gorton AFC moved to Hyde Road in 1887, it wasn't until 1889 that the first stadium was built there. In fact, the only person from the club's formative years still active in Manchester football at this time was Walter Chew who, as treasurer of the Manchester FA, would have had close dealings with Allison. Chew is also recorded as helping Fred Johnson with his 1930 history. The claim that a "W. Chew" was "the father of the club", may indicate that Chew saw the founding of West Gorton Association (which he captained) as City's starting point. However, there may also have been a political motive behind that claim.

The *Book of Football* was published on 23 March 1906, when City were being investigated by the FA over allegations of illegal payments to players. A week earlier Allison, along with other directors, had testified for nearly four hours in front of the FA's commission. Two years earlier the FA had suspended five City directors after an investigation into the transfer of a player, and linking a senior FA official to the club so closely may have been an attempt to ease the impending sanctions. If it was, it did not succeed. On 31 May 1906 the FA handed out the harshest punishments ever seen in English football. Allison, four directors and a former chairman were suspended, manager Tom Maley was banned for life and seventeen players were suspended for 19 months.

This then leaves the 1898 *Golden Penny* as probably the most reliable source. Written just 14 years after the event, and published by the man who owned most of Britain's sporting press, it is certainly the one that is most is in line with recently-uncovered evidence. So, with the creation of Gorton Association established as City's starting point, is it now possible to identity the club's founding fathers?

The Footballers' Football Club

The creation of Gorton Association was funded largely by a £5 donation from locomotive manufacturer Richard Peacock. That would have covered the £3 15s rent for the ground and dressing room plus the 10s 6d subscription to the Manchester FA, leaving 14s 6d remaining for "football requisites". Peacock was a key member of Manchester's Mechanic Institute movement, which had already helped the spread of working men's team sport, and his iron works had created Gorton's first working-class cricket club in 1865. However, no evidence exists of Peacock having a direct involvement with the new club outside his donation. He was renowned for his generosity, so much so that in 1885 Rev. Josiah Bennett from the Free Church in Openshaw referred contemptuously to the "mob of pensioners, spongers and hangers-on at Gorton Hall" (Peacock's home). Indeed, as Peacock had already announced his intention to stand in the upcoming General Election, he may have just been used as an easy source of funds by the founding players.

At the end-of-season club dinner former St Mark's church officials James Moores and William Beastow presided. Both had actively promoted team sport in the district for some years. Beastow had been chairman of St Mark's cricket club and, according to the *Gorton Reporter*, both he and Moores had encouraged local young men to take up sports such as cricket and football during a talk at St Mark's in April 1882. Although it's possible that they played a role in Gorton Association's creation the best clue to the club's origins can be found in the *Gorton Reporter*. On 25 October 1884 it stated that

> "The members of the old West Gorton Association
> Football Club have pulled together, and, with the
> assistance of a few other players, have formed a
> new club under the name of "Gorton Association".
> A suitable ground has been secured near Belle Vue
> station. Mr E Kitchen, railway cottages, Longsight
> has been appointed secretary. He is staging matches
> for both first and second teams."

This indicates that the players themselves were the driving force behind the club, which tallies with the *Golden Penny's* claim that "a number of young men" formed the club. The end of season accounts, which reveal the payment of membership fees, also points to this being a club run by its players. The "old West Gorton Association" club was the one that was first recorded playing in the 1882-83 season. According to *Athletic News*, "several" of its old players had helped establish the new club. Some had previously played for St Mark's and now, with five years' of footballing experience to draw from, they became a driving force behind Gorton AFC's creation. The club's first secretary, 22-year-old clerk Edward Kitchen, had been a regular for St Mark's since their opening match in 1880, one which the Gorton AFC's probable treasurer, Frederick Hopkinson, also played in.

The captain, W Turner, would have also played an important role in the club's early days, particularly as he was a university student, which at that time conferred a much higher social status compared to the others. Another figure who may have been instrumental in the club's formation is 26-year-old Lawrence Furniss, who had recently arrived in Gorton from Cromford, Derbyshire. Probably the most experienced footballer in Gorton, Furniss had served as captain of Cromford Football Club in 1877 and had also played for Matlock FC. He moved to the United States some time after April 1882 but had returned to Derbyshire by October 1883. The following month he was a referee for Matlock FC and some time after that moved to Gorton. Furniss is also holding the football on the only team photo taken that season, suggesting seniority over the other players.

Warehouse clerk Walter Chew, who had captained Belle Vue Rangers, St Mark's and West Gorton Association during the 1882-83 season, was also likely to have been a driving force along with his elder brother, William, who served as the club's umpire that season. However, the fact that Walter Chew was not captain of the new club suggests that he was not the central figure in its creation. According to the 1881 census a warehouse boy called William Lee lived a few doors down from the Chews at 21 Elizabeth Street. He was the same age as Walter Chew and is probably the person mentioned in the *Golden Penny*. It's unclear why he was credited as being the club's first secretary instead of Kitchen, but it's possible the two shared the role (when the club renamed itself Ardwick in 1887 it initially had two secretaries). Another possibility is that he was the first secretary of West Gorton Association in 1882-83. His name also injects one last drop of scandal into the City story. His father, Thomas Lee, listed as a clerk for a "Liberal Association" in the 1881 census, had been charged with embezzlement in January 1880.

What exactly brought these seven young men together is unclear. There were certainly many ties to the St Mark's parish. However, given the problem the Church faced over retaining young male parishioners during this period, there is no evidence that this was a unifying bond. Indeed, Gorton AFC officials Moores and Beastow had both severed their official ties with St Mark's in April 1884. The pair, along with rector's warden Edwin Reynolds, had decided not to stand for re-election that month. The reasons are not clear but comments by Arthur Connell during the church elections, which referred to "persons who were never happy except when creating diversions, causing feelings of animosity to arise, and making parties in the parish", suggest the church had been hit by in-fighting.

In fact, such is the complex nature of human interaction that establishing common bonds is problematical. Like all organisations it probably had cliques, most likely based on where they were schooled, worked, played and prayed. A shared social status is noticeable, with five of the seven senior players listed as clerks in the 1881 census. It's also worth noting that all of the available evidence points to this being a club made up exclusively of Protestant men, a fact that would have been instantly recognised in the ethnically-divided Gorton. That is not at all surprising given the history of association football up until this point. This was an almost exclusively Protestant pastime, with a work ethic to match.

A local iron works link is noticeable. As well as Peacock and Beastow's involvement, four members of the first recorded line-up were iron workers. And, as we'll discover in the next chapter, the only club photo from Gorton AFC's first season includes the owner of the Union Iron works and his son. There also appears to have been a grouping of warehouse employees. Both Chew brothers were warehouse clerks and by 3 January warehousemen Edward Groves and John Fletcher had joined the side. The pair, along with Kitchen, had also appeared in the same Belle Vue line-up on 27 January 1883, a side that Chew captained.

Maps from this period show that the only major warehouses in the area were located at Belle Vue pleasure gardens. Lawrence Furniss, who was a clerk for the Midland Railway in Cromford, may also have worked at the company's Belle Vue station, which was close-by. A Belle Vue connection might also explain how W Turner became involved in the club. Dalton Hall, for whom he played, occasionally staged home fixtures near the gardens. Further research may uncover a common link to a workplace, or to a political society or social club. However, sometimes the best answer is also the simplest one.

There were three types of football clubs formed in the sport's early days. Church teams, such as St Mark's, were created to instill a "Muscular" Christianity in young men. Works teams, such as Newton Heath, reflected the owners' abhorrence of idleness and alcoholic excess. But Gorton Association represented another type of club, one created and run by the players themselves.

And these young men shared a common bond that probably overrode all others: a love of the game of football.

Gorton AFC first recorded line-up, 22 November 1884

Name	Previous clubs
Joseph Payton	**West Gorton** 1883-84 (3 games) **Belle Vue** 1882-83 (4 games)
Edward Bower	**West Gorton** 1883-84 (4 games) **Belle Vue** 1882-83 (6 games)
Frederick Hopkinson	**St Mark's** 1880-83 (12 games)
Lawrence Prenty	
Avery	**Belle Vue** 1882 (1 game)
Edward Kitchen	**West Gorton Association** 1883 **St Mark's** 1880-83 (21 games) **Belle Vue** 1883 (1 game)
W Turner (captain)	**Dalton Hall**
Owen	
Walter Chew	**West Gorton** 1883-84 (2 games) **West Gorton Association** 1883 (captain) **Belle Vue** 1882-83 (5 games as captain) **St Mark's** 1881-83 (2 or more games)
J Booth	**West Gorton** 1884 (1 game)
J Mellor	

New football clubs in the Manchester area 1881-82

First known appearance	Club	Home ground	Origins
15 Oct 1881	Bentfield	Greenfield	Bentfield Mill cricket team
19 Oct 1881	Hurst Clarence	Ashton-under-Lyne	Possibly mill works team
14 Jan 1882	Haughton Dale Rovers	Haughton Dale	Possibly Clarence Mill works team
14 Jan 1882	Belle Vue Rangers	Queen's Road, West Gorton	Possibly Rifle Volunteers or YMCA
14 Jan 1882	Hurst Park Road	Ashton (near infirmary)	
Feb 1882	Marple	Marple	
Feb 1882	Hooley Hill Rovers	Audenshaw	

New football clubs in the Manchester area 1882-83

First known appearance	Club	Home ground	Origins
14 Oct 1882	Gorton Tank Rovers	Probably Openshaw Park	MSL Railway iron works
Oct 1882	Greenheys	Dog Kennel Lane, Moss Side	Coupland St Presbyterian Church
11 Nov 1882	Hurst Brook Olympic	Ashton-under-Lyne	Possibly Mechanics Institute
11 Nov 1882	Denton Association	Denton	Probably members club
6 Jan 1883	Uppermill Congregational	Probably near Greenfield station	Ebenezer Congregational Church
20 Jan 1883	Hurst Lees Street Rangers	Ashton-under-Lyne	
24 Feb 1883	West Gorton Association	Possibly beside Union Iron works, West Gorton	Probably members club
1883	Heaton Norris Rovers	Stockport	Wycliffe Congregional Church

New clubs in the Manchester area 1883 to Oct 1884

First known appearance	Club	Home ground	Origins
Sep 1883	Heywood Rovers	Heywood	Formed out of failed rugby club
Sep 1883	Pendleton Olympic	Whit Lane, Pendleton	Possibly Mechanics Institute
6 Oct 1883	Hurdsfield	Macclesfield	
13 Oct 1883	Furness Vale	Furness Vale	
1883-84	Dalton Hall	Dog Kennel Lane, Moss Side	Owens College
Nov 1883	Thornham	Thornham	
16 Dec 1883	Tame Valley Rangers	Stalybridge	
1884	Heywood St James	Heywood	
12 Jan 1884	Levenshulme	Levenshulme	Possibly Birch reformed
22 Mar 1884	Gorton Villa	Gorton	Possibly Gorton Mills team
Sep 1884	Eccles	Eccles	
25 Oct 1884	Gorton Association	Pink Bank Lane, Longsight	Members club

The men who created Gorton Association FC

Name	Age	Position at club	Profession (1)	Previous clubs
Edward Kitchen	22	Secretary	Clerk	St Mark's FC Belle Vue Rangers
Lawrence Furniss	26	Probably on committee	Probably railway clerk	Cromford FC Cromford CC Matlock FC West Gorton CC
Frederick Hopkinson	21	Probably treasurer	Clerk	St Mark's Juniors St Mark's FC
W Turner		Captain	Student	Dalton Hall
William Chew	22	Umpire	Warehouse clerk	St Mark's Juniors St Mark's FC
Walter Chew	19	Probably on committee	Warehouse clerk	St Mark's Juniors St Mark's FC Belle Vue Rangers West Gorton Assoc. West Gorton FC
William Lee (2)		Possibly joint secretary	Warehouseboy	

(1) Professions as listed in 1881 census
(2) No contemporary account of involvement

CHAPTER 6

THE MALTESE CROSS PHOTOGRAPH: MYSTERY SOLVED?

It is an iconic image for City fans, though one that for years has been shrouded in mystery. But now the names of the men in Gorton AFC's 1884-85 team photograph, and the reason the players wore a Maltese Cross on their shirts, can be revealed.

The key to unlocking its secrets was an observation by Paul Toovey, author of *Birth of the Blues*. He noticed that the players were arranged in the same order as their 2-3-5 team formation. The identities of three players, Walter Chew (back row, left), Lawrence Furniss (middle row, centre) and Edward Kitchen (middle row, right), can be established by looking at later photographs of them. And there was only one game that season where Chew, Furniss and Kitchen were listed in these exact positions: the Manchester & District Challenge Cup tie with Dalton Hall on 31 January 1885.

Here is the line-up for that match, indicating the position of the players in the photograph:

Walter Chew, R Hopkinson, D Melville, T Kirk, J Bain
E Groves, L Furniss, E Kitchen
K Mackenzie, F Hopkinson
I Bower

In regards to the players, that only leaves the mystery of the 12th man (located on right of the back row). The most likely candidate is William Chew, Walter's older brother, who was one of the umpires that day. Another possibility is John Beastow, who played in St Mark's first match in 1880 and who bears a resemblance to the figure to the right of him, his father William Beastow.

Gorton Association Football Club 1884-85

Here are the details of the 12 players:

Front row (left to right)

Kenneth Mackenzie (captain)
The 17-year-old made his debut on 6 December, replacing Turner as captain (Turner never played for Gorton again and the reason for the switch is unclear). Mackenzie didn't play for the club in the next two seasons, when the home ground was on the eastern boundary of Gorton, but he later became a regular for Ardwick, making at least 25 appearances between 1887-1890. Mackenzie appears to have been born in Liverpool, the son of an accountant living in Toxteth Park. According to the 1891 census he married Sarah Baronda, a member of a Mexican-American land-owning family who had arrived in Britain in unknown circumstances.

Isaac Bower (goalkeeper)
The 26-year-old joiner was born in Mottram, Cheshire and moved to West Gorton aged around nine. The son of a provision dealer living at 251 Hyde Road, Bower was a former St Mark's player who made his first appearance for them in November 1881. Initially a forward, he replaced Kitchen in goal two months after his St Mark's debut. He may have played at No.5 for Gorton AFC on 6 December before again replacing Kitchen as goalkeeper the following game. It's likely that his younger brother, 21-year-old Edward Bower (described as a "great full-back with mighty kick in either foot") played in Gorton's first recorded line-up on 22 November, before being replaced by Mackenzie.

Frederick Hopkinson
The 21-year-old clerk lived at 71 Clowes Street and read out the annual report at Gorton's end of season dinner. He was the secretary of St Mark's Juniors cricket club (1878-80) and may have been secretary of its football club. The son of the church's organist, Hopkinson was also a member of its choral society.

Middle row players (left to right)

Edward Groves
The 21-year-old warehouseman from Ardwick was described as the best player for the Cup tie against Dalton Hall. Manchester-born with a Welsh mother, Groves played his first game for St Mark's in February 1881 and became a regular for both West Gorton and Belle Vue between 1881-1884. He continued to play for Gorton for the next two seasons and also played for Ardwick in 1887-88.

Lawrence Furniss
The 26-year-old was unquestionably the most influential person in the club's history. Over the next four decades – spanning Gorton's transition into Ardwick and rebirth as Manchester City FC – he served as captain, manager, director and chairman, a feat which may be unique in professional football.

Furniss was born in Cromford, Derbyshire early in 1858, the eldest child of station master Edwin Furniss and wife Sarah. In 1881 he worked with his father as a clerk at Cromford's Midland Railway station. By that time he had become the village's most prominent sportsman, serving as captain and committee member of the Cromford Football Club and captain and secretary of its Cricket Club. In November 1881 he is also recorded as playing for nearby Matlock Football Club.

Furniss moved to the United States some time after April 1882 and is recorded as playing in three cricket matches there. In June 1883 he played twice for the Merion Cricket Club, whose ground is located beside the Merion railway station on the outskirts of Philadelphia. The following month he is recorded as playing for a cricket team called English Residents v American Born at the Germantown Cricket Club Ground in Nicetown, Philadelphia.

He had returned to Derbyshire by October 1883 and that month was a referee for Matlock Football Club. He moved to Gorton some time between November 1883 and June 1884 and soon became an active member of the community. In the summer of 1884 he played for the West Gorton Cricket Club and by 1900 had become a warden at St Mark's.

After retiring as Gorton captain in 1886 because of injury he joined the club's committee and in 1887 helped them secure a new ground off Hyde Road, Ardwick. In 1889 he became manager of the renamed Ardwick AFC and for the next four years oversaw their transition from small amateur club to Football League members. A director of Manchester City when they won the FA Cup in 1904, he was appointed chairman in May 1920, a position he held for the next nine seasons. During that time the club moved to Maine Road, finished second in the League and reached an FA Cup final and semi-final.

Edward Kitchen

The 22-year-old clerk was a regular for St Mark's during its first three seasons and also played a game for Belle Vue. Born in Bramhall, Cheshire, the engine driver's son lived at 4 Tank Row (also known as Railway Cottages). He was baptised by Rev. Adams at the original St Mark's in November 1864, and married at the new St Mark's church in 1887.

Back row players (left to right)

Walter Chew

A 19-year-old warehouse clerk who lived at 12 Elizabeth St (off Clowes Street), Chew was to play a critical role in Gorton AFC's development. In the 1885-86 season he took over from Kitchen as club secretary and also played in games. In January 1887 he began negotiations with the MSL Railway company that led to the club securing the Hyde Road ground in Ardwick, one that became City's home until 1923. In August that year he was listed as Hon. Sec. Pro Tem (along with J H Ward) when the formation of Ardwick Association Football Club was announced and was match secretary for 1887-88 season. A 1900 *Golden Penny* article described him as one of the prime movers of Ardwick AFC while in 1910 the *Manchester Guardian* called him the founder of the Ardwick club. Chew became a member of the Manchester FA in 1888-89 and was appointed treasurer in 1903. In January 1910 he was presented with the long-service medal for his services to Manchester football.

Richard Hopkinson

The 24-year-old clerk lived with younger brother, Frederick, and his father. He had played for St Mark's in its first three seasons and was also a keen cricketer, opening the batting for the Gorton Tradesmen side in 1884. A member of the church's choral society, he was probably the Mr R Hopkinson listed as a conductor for the Gorton Philharmonic orchestra in 1904.

D Melville

No details available

Thomas Kirk

The 22-year-old velvet buyer's assistant lived at 18, Gorton Lane. He was born in Manchester.

J Bain

No details available

William Chew (identity not confirmed)

The 22-year old Chew, a founding St Mark's player, served as Gorton's umpire for the 1884-85 season. In 1886 he became Gorton AFC's treasurer and was one of four men on the club management committee that season. In August 1887 he was one of the four names on the tenancy agreement for the new ground in Ardwick and served on the club's 12-man committee for the first season.

The Men in Suits

The identities of the well-dressed gentleman in the photograph have also caused much inquiry over the years. While it was likely that club president James Moores was the figure standing on the left, and vice-president William Beastow the figure on the right, the two other well-dressed men were something of a mystery, particularly as the seated position of the snappily-dressed young man on the left signified a higher social rank than

Moores and Beastow.

It is clear that careful thought went into the taking of this photograph. The heights of the men in the back row form an arc, while the heads of the three men on the right are at right-angles to the three on the left. The symmetry even extents to the folded arms of six of the players. Indeed, this photograph is better-crafted than those of more successful sports teams during this period. It would also have been expensive to create, particularly as it was taken outside the studio. As the cost of the photograph was not included in the club's accounts for that season, it was probably paid for by one of the well-dressed men. Club donor Richard Peacock would be the most likely candidate, particularly as he had a long white beard similar to the man seated on the right. However, a closer examination of a photograph of Peacock taken around this time revealed very different facial features.

The mystery looked to remain unsolved until I came across a newspaper report detailing a social event that had taken place in West Gorton on Christmas Eve 1884. It revealed that a substantial tea had been laid on in St Mark's schoolroom to celebrate the 21st birthday of Samuel Herbert Brooks, the only son of Union Iron founder Samuel Brooks. To mark the occasion Brooks snr had also donated a costly altar cloth, hangings, lectern and reading desk to the church. In Gorton's next match, on 3 January 1884, a player named Brooks is listed as playing his only game for the club. A photograph of Samuel H Brooks from 1895 reveals a good likeness to the man seated on the left of the picture. Brooks had lived in France and "travelled extensively" throughout the United States and Europe, which might explain his American-style clothing and French-style goatee beard.

It's possible that the photograph was part of S H Brooks jnr's coming of age celebrations, which served as his introduction to Gorton working life and were designed to help prepare him for his upcoming role of employer and social guardian (Brooks snr died 22 months later). This was the first time that a Gorton sports club had played in a Cup competition, and a commemorative photograph would have marked the pride felt by both the workers and the employers of the area.

Owing to the lack of alternative candidates, I have concluded that the bearded man sitting on the right is probably his father, Samuel Brooks, who was Beastow's employer at Union Iron. Brooks was a farmer's son, which is consistent with this man's large frame, while the thinness of his face also tallies with the fact that he had been battling health problems for some time. Further evidence of a Brooks connection is found in the club's accounts from the 1885-86 season, which reveal a £1 1s donation from S. Brooks Esq.

The photograph was probably taken outside the Brooks's family home, Slade House, in Levenshulme. It was roughly 1.5 miles from where the match was played and would have been a convenient stop-off point for players travelling from West Gorton. Although it's also possible that the photograph was taken outside Dalton Hall (which lay a mile from the ground), the fact that Brooks snr was in poor health at this time means it is unlikely he'd want to take a carriage ride on a winter's day for a photograph that he was probably paying for.

Here are who I believe to be the four suited men in the photograph:

James Moores, chairman (standing left)
The 43-year-old ran a hat shop from Denton House on Gorton Lane, where he lived with his wife, two daughters and mother-in-law. He was probably a member of the family that owned the J & T Moores hat works in Denton, which employed 1,100 people in 1892. Active in Conservative politics, he was a member of the Gorton Local Board for most of the 1880s and was elected councillor for Gorton's St Clements Ward in April 1884. He was also the elected sidesman at St Mark's between April 1881 and April 1884. He died on 27 May 1891, aged 50.

Samuel Herbert Brooks (seated left)
The 21-year-old Brooks was to have a long association with the Gorton area. Born on Christmas Day 1863, he was educated at the Moravian school in Fairfield and later served an apprenticeship with S Walker in Lille, France. He took charge of

Union Iron following the sudden death of his father in December 1886 and soon expanded the firm. In April 1888 he bought Junction Iron Works, Newton Heath from its liquidators and operated it as a branch establishment, employing 500 staff. In January 1892 the firm was renamed Brooks & Doxey (after Richard Alexander Doxey became a partner), and Brooks was its chairman when it was floated in 1898.

Brooks's ties with St Mark's remained strong after his father's death, and in April 1888 the Rev. Connell appointed him warden, replacing Union Iron manager Thomas Goodbehere. Brooks was also a councillor for the St Mark's ward between 1893 and 1898, chairman of Gorton's fire brigade (and a very popular one according to an 1899 biography), chairman of the Gorton's Conservative Association and its Registration Committee. He was also a captain in the 4th Manchester Volunteer Batallion and in December 1902 was appointed a magistrate.

According to the 1899 publication *Contemporary Biographies*, Brooks was "an all-round sportsman who enjoyed shooting, fishing, hunting, yachting, lacrosse etc" and the owner of a valuable collection of books. Good-looking, well-travelled, sporting, learned and rich, he was undoubtedly the most eligible bachelor in Gorton, though he waited for the 20th century to arrive before tying the knot. On 25 August 1900 William Beastow was one of the members of the Gorton Division Conservative Registration Committee who presented him with a "massive silver " to mark his approaching marriage.

Samuel Brooks (seated right)

The quintessential Victorian self-made man, Samuel Brooks was born in Middleton-by-Wirksworth, Derbyshire around 1826, roughly a mile from where Lawrence Furniss was born. The son of a farmer, he was educated at the local Grammar school and began work as a draughtsman for eminent German Swiss engineer Johan Bodmer, who built locomotives and cotton machinery at his works off Oxford Street, Manchester. After a spell at Ancoats cotton machinery manufacturers, John Elce & Co, Brooks set up his own cotton machinery works in 1859 at

Union Mills off London Road. Initially he engaged "but one man and several boys", but business expanded rapidly and in 1864 he moved to more extensive premises on Thomas Street in West Gorton.

Union Iron soon became one of the world's leading manufacturers of cotton machinery. By 1880 it had around 700 employees, which grew to nearly 900 by 1883. Two years later the firm won gold medals at the International Inventions Exhibition in London and the Universelle Exposition, Antwerp, as well as a silver medal at the World's Fair in New Orleans.

Although Brooks had close ties with St Mark's, it's unclear what his exact religious beliefs were. His son was educated by Moravians, who believed in working within existing Protestant denominations, or even among people who were unattached to any church, to enhance spiritual life.

Politically Liberal, he was president of St Clements Liberal Club in Longsight when it opened its new headquarters in May 1886. However, he was known as someone who "devoted himself almost exclusively to his business" and according to the *Manchester Courier*

> "Although a Liberal in politics, he seldom took any
> active part in the promotion of those political
> principles he professed, and what little effort he did
> make in this respect was confined to the district
> where he was known so well".

He still found time to serve on the Gorton Local Board for several years and according to a newspaper obituary "held other offices in district Liberal institutions". Brooks's wife died in 1882 and by the time this photo was taken he "had not enjoyed the best of health for some time". On Monday 7 December 1886 he attended a meeting at St Mark's where the Rev. Connell was presented with a marble clock and purse of gold from parishioners to mark his 21 years at the church. The following morning Brooks was found dead in his bed at Slade House, Levenshulme, aged 60. He was buried at Southern cemetery on

18 December. Connell officiated at his funeral, which saw 500 employees walk in front of the hearse.

William Henry Beastow, vice-chairman (standing, right)
The 49-year-old was foreman at Samuel Brooks's Union Iron Works – and the most active member of public life in Gorton.

Manchester-born Beastow was elected to the Gorton Local Board in 1879. In an era before free heath care and state benefits, taking care of the sick and the poor provided huge headaches for public officials, but Beastow was always in the front line of efforts to alleviate hardships. He was a member of the relief committee set up to deal with the effects of the savage economic depression in the winter of 1878, and in 1880 was the driving force behind the creation of the Gorton Provident Dispensary (a clinic offering medical care to people who made a small weekly payment). In 1882 he was appointed overseer to the poor, holding the position for 25 years, and in 1895 organised the fundraising efforts of St Mark's ragged school, which taught the poorest children of the district.

It's possible that tragedies in his personal life had made him more sympathetic to the plight of others. The 1851 census shows him as being married to Harriet Ellen Beastow. Both were just 15-years-old, which was highly unusual even in Victorian times (the law allowed for girls from the age of 12 to marry and boys from the age of 14. Prior to 1858 there had been no minimum age. In 1875 the age of consent for girls was raised to 13, and remained unchanged until 1929). The 1861 census records him being married to Jane Alice Beastow and living on Hyde Road. As divorce was practically impossible to obtain in those days, his first wife had presumably died. In 1869 tragedy struck a second time when Jane Alice died, aged just 34. Beastow later moved to Clowes Street, West Gorton with his third wife, Charlotte, son John 19, daughter Emily Alice 21, and 19-year-old step-son Charles Frederick.

He had enjoyed close ties with St Mark's, and is believed to have helped establish its working men's meetings in 1879 as well as serving as chairman of its cricket club. He was elected sidesman at St Mark's in 1879 and was elevated to the position of parishioners' warden in 1881. However, after announcing that he was not seeking re-election in 1884, no further official ties with the church are recorded.

Beastow's public life also shadowed Samuel Herbert Brooks's. In 1898 he was elected Conservative councillor for the St Mark's ward after Brooks stepped down, and was appointed a magistrate on the same day as Brooks on 31 December 1902.

He was undoubtedly a well-liked man. In 1880, during a lecture he chaired on the Scotch Covenanters at the Primitive Methodist chapel, he was described by Rev. A Morton as a man of "great kindness and geniality of disposition". This may partly explain his popularity with voters. In 1898 he beat ILP candidate W H Griffiths by 1,231 votes to 420 – the biggest margin in any local council contest that year.

He was also capable of making the occasional rousing speech. At a meeting of the conservative Primrose League in August 1903 he exhorted members to be ready for a fight and get their armour ready to be buckled on at short notice. The indefatigable Beastow was without doubt a man who practised what he preached.

In 1905 he was listed as the general treasurer of the Rational Friendly Society and by this time had moved to Birch Cottage, Lime Grove, Longsight. He was also a long-serving member of the Ashbury's Masonic Lodge (no. 1459), making him the first in a long line of Freemasons who have shaped the fortunes of Manchester City FC.

The Maine Road Connection

Unbeknown to the assembled side, the location of the match against Dalton Hall was a place that would later have great football significance. It was played on Dog Kennel Lane, also known as Maine Road, the home of Manchester City FC from 1923 to 2003.

It's not clear exactly when Maine Road got its name. By 1876 it was designated as "Domain Road" on ordnance survey maps – a translation of the French word "Demesne", which was the name of a nearby farm – but was also being referred to as Dog Kennel Lane in newspapers. At a meeting of the Moss Side Local Board that September the local Temperance Society proposed the name be officially changed to Domain Road, but after opposition "the matter was adjourned for further consideration". Soon afterwards abbreviated forms of "Domain" were commonly used for the road's name. As the pronunciation of "Domain Road" sounds similar to "the Main Road", the "Do-" was probably dropped in order to avoid confusion. The earliest record of it being called Maine Road was on 24 March 1879, and the same spelling was recorded in the 1881 census. But it was usually referred to as Main Road in newspaper reports until 1893. According to a theory in Gary James's *Big Book of City*, the "e" spelling was adopted in order to commemorate the 1851 "Maine Law" – the first to prohibit alcohol in a US state – though the source of the claim is unknown.

The Maine Road ground was probably on the land adjoining Pepperhill Farm where Manchester Association first played in 1875, and most likely the same ground where the reformed Manchester Association Wanderers are recorded as playing on 19 November 1881 (below). This would have been on the north-western side of Maine Road, close to where Manchester City's stadium was later built.

MANCHESTER WANDERERS (2ND TEAM) v. MIDDLETON (ASSOCIATION).—This match was played on the Wanderers' ground, Maine-road, Moss Side, and resulted after an hour's play, in a win for the home team by three goals to none.

The Mystery of the Maltese Cross

Probably the biggest mystery surrounding the team photograph is the origin and possible meaning of the Maltese Cross on the black shirts. To date, many theories have been advanced. David Winner's *Those Feet: A Sensual History of English Football* claimed it was the symbol of the White Cross Society, a temperance organisation created by social reformer Ellice Hopkins. Unfortunately Winner was unable to offer evidence to back up the claim. Another theory is tied up with the figure of William Beastow who, according to Andrew Ward's *The Manchester City Story*, presented the kit to the players. That later led to speculation that the shirts had Masonic significance, though no evidence has yet materialised to support the claim, or indeed, to indicate that Beastow had supplied the shirts.

The Cross in Popular Use

Technically speaking the shape is called a "cross pattee" (though was often referred to as a Maltese Cross in the Victorian era) and was a commonly-used design during this period. It is the same design as the Victoria Cross, which would have been instantly recognisable thanks to the widespread reporting of military campaigns. Sixteen VCs were awarded during the Afghan War of 1878-1880, 23 during the 1879 Anglo-Zulu War, and five during the campaign in the Sudan in 1884-85. The cross pattee design would have been familiar in a non-military context too. It can still be seen in the brickwork facade of Longsight's largest warehouse during this period and even appeared on a Manchester ginger beer bottle.

Moreover, the cross pattee already had great significance in the sports world of late Victorian England, including football. Many examples exist of the Maltese Cross being used by sports teams in public school and universities. For instance Donald Leinster-Mackay's *The Rise of the English Prep School* describes rugby players at St George's Ascot wearing a light blue cap with a silver Maltese Cross on it. The 1868 *Sketches of Club-life, Hunting and Sports* has a reference to the St Anthony's College

Oxford rowing team which wore a red Maltese cross on a white background, while Routledge's *Every Boy's Annual* from the following year describes Old Boys' football teams using Maltese cross house insignia.

But the symbol first became connected to modern-day football when Blackburn Rovers used it on their shirts some time after their formation in 1875. One of the co-founders of Blackburn Rovers was Arthur Constantine, a former pupil of Shrewsbury School. It's possible he copied the design from the school's rowing team, who still use it to this day.

At this time Blackburn footballing matters had great significance in English football circles. Blackburn Rovers won the FA Cup in 1884, and in the following two years. Indeed, the influence of Blackburn's exploits on Manchester football can be seen in the aftermath of the first Manchester Cup final in 1885, in which Hurst beat Newton Heath 3-0 at Whalley Range. The victorious players had retired to the Pitt & Nelson pub after the match where the landlord, Joseph Fletcher, made a speech. According to *The Reporter* newspaper, Fletcher declared that he

> "Had been to Blackburn recently and he could
> assure them that the fame of the Hurst club was well
> known in that district and that he was certain that
> the next season they would be called upon to play
> with teams from that district, the Mother of the
> Game."

According to some club histories, Tottenham Hotspurs's players adopted Blackburn's shirt design, including a cross pattee, after watching them in the 1884 FA Cup final. The cross pattee was also adopted by Earlestown AFC, who reached the final of the Liverpool Cup in 1884 and won it the following year, though the only picture of them wearing a cross was taken after the Liverpool Cup win in the spring of 1885. Until recently the Earlestown connection was the most promising lead, particularly as both Gorton and Earlestown were centres of the iron and railway locomotive industry.

Manchester's Footballing Cousins?

Another possible lead emerged in the shape of the Lancashire & Yorkshire Railway. A blue and red cross pattee insignia was used by the Goole Steam Shipping Company, which started a channel ferry service in 1879. The ferry port was served exclusively by the L & YR, which bought Goole Steam Shipping in 1904 and used a black and white insignia on its ships' flags. Gorton Association's financial backer, Richard Peacock, had close ties with the L & Y, building 50 locomotives for them in 1881-82.

The insignia of Goole Steam Shipping, early 1900s

The idea that this may represent one of the earliest examples of shirt advertising is a fascinating one, as is the idea that City share a common railway ancestry with Manchester United, who were originally a LYR carriage works team. It also may be significant that all of Gorton's opponents during the 1884-85 season were served by stations on LYR lines. However, until concrete evidence is found tying the shirt design to the ferry company, the theory remains a speculative one.

A New Explanation

In September 1866 the *Courier* revealed that the Manchester

Mechanics Institute Gymnastics Club had awarded medals at its annual contest "in the form of a Maltese Cross with the Manchester arms in the centre, surrounded with a band inscribed with the name of the club". As the traditional eight-pointed Maltese Cross (also called the Amalfi cross) would not have enough surface area for inscriptions, the Institute medals could only practicably have been a pattee cross design.

Since its creation in 1825 the Manchester Institute had gone to great lengths to recruit young men from the upper working classes. According to its 1836 annual report, 756 of its 1,526 members were 21-years-old or younger. Broken down by types of employment, the second largest group were clerks (who accounted for 19% of the membership) followed by warehousemen (13%). Indeed, membership of the Mechanics Institute consisted of precisely the type of young men assembled for the team photograph. The man holding the ball in the team photograph, Lawrence Furniss, had been an active member of the Derbyshire Mechanics Institute, and it's possible that other players were members of the movement too.

The Mechanics Institute certainly played an important role in the lives of Gorton AFC's senior figures. Peacock was president of the Manchester Mechanics Institute when Gorton AFC's team photograph was taken, and also president of its Openshaw, Bradford and Gorton branch. Samuel Brooks and his son were members, as was William Beastow. The fact that four of the five most prominent people in the photograph, as well as the club's main donor, share membership of the same sports-promoting organisation probably influenced the choice of shirt design. However, such was the prevalence of the Maltese Cross in Manchester life during this period the exact reasons for it appearing on the jerseys will always be open to doubt. In 2012 I discovered a commemorative medal marking the 100th anniversary of Manchester Sunday schools in 1880 (pictured p127). It also had the Manchester arms in the centre surrounded by a band carrying an inscription. It's possible that the St Mark's contingent at the club had received these medals. On 24 August 1880, less than three months before the creation of its football club, St Mark's celebrated the anniversary of its Sunday school.

According to a newspaper report, "in the afternoon the Sunday School scholars met at the schoolroom and, decorated with centenary medals, walked in procession to the church". However, the report does not describe the shape of the medals.

As the cross pattee was not associated with any Manchester churches at this time it's unlikely the 1880 medal had any particular religious significance. The handing out of medals was a common occurrence in Sunday schools, and represented little more than an inducement for the young men to remain there. In 1887 Manchester and Salford Sunday Schools issued another cross pattee medal, to commemorate Queen Victoria's Golden Jubilee. Its design differed slightly to the 1880 medal, and probably provides the best clue to the cross pattee's popularity.

The medal was the exact shape of the Victoria Cross, the British Army's highest military decoration for valour. The award of the VC was usually accompanied by widespread newspaper coverage. Astonishing accounts of heroism, such as the Battle of Rorke's Drift in January 1879 (which resulted in eleven VCs being awarded) captured the public's imagination That in turn helped the army to recruit young men. Indeed, the Victoria Cross design was also used as the insignia of some Volunteer Rifle regiments during this period. All of which provides us with a thread that binds the cross pattee to the Mechanics Institute, the military and the game of football.

In July 1869 the inaugural Longsight Athletics Festival took place on land to the south of Belle Vue, a few hundred yards from Gorton AFC's Pink Bank Lane ground. It was organised by the Manchester Mechanics Institute's sister organisation, the Manchester Athenaeum, which had played a key role in the promotion of working men's sport. At the festival, the honorary secretary of the Athenaeum, William Romaine Callender, revealed just how close the bond between early football and the military had been. He declared that "the love of field sports" had been so productive "the volunteer movement itself might be traced to it". By the 1880s the volunteer movement had become an important part of Gorton life. Richard Peacock's son, Ralph, was the commanding officer of the 7th Lancashire Artillery Volunteers – which were based on Hyde Road, close to Gorton

AFC's ground – while Samuel Brooks jnr later became a captain in the 4th Manchester Volunteer Battalion.

Moral and Mental

But for men like Romaine Callender the promotion of the military was a means, not an end. In 1836 the aims of the Manchester Mechanics Institute were laid out by its president, Benjamin Heywood. Chief among them was the desire "to diffuse useful information among the working classes.. to draw them from scenes of dissipation and vice, by furnishing them with rational employment for their leisure". Thirty years later William Callender spelled out what this entailed in an 1869 speech.

"No person could be a member of that club unless he was prepared to undergo a course of moral discipline which must be valuable to him as regarded health and his future prospects, and the mere fact of their exercising self-denial at an early age could not fail to have in the future most valuable influence on the after life of the matured man".

That self-denial would have required abstinence from alcohol, gambling and masturbation. But in the minds of Manchester's social engineers, the reward was a noble one. In his 1836 speech, Benjamin Heywood spelled out the Institute's ultimate aims: "Real happiness and elevation of character in this life" and preparation for "a higher, a nobler, and a holier state of being". He noted that near St Peter's church in Rome there were "two lofty and lovely fountains". These, he declared, were "the two most beautiful fountains in the world", and the Manchester Athenaeum, along with its twin organisation, the Mechanics Institute, were "equally useful and equally permanent". He continued: "Both diffuse around them, like intellectual fountains, the refreshing influence of moral and mental improvement."

Arthur Connell, who once gave a lecture called "The moral and mental improvement of young men", was fighting a similar cause. The rector of Gorton's Unitarian church, S A Steinthal, was also an active member of both the Mechanics Institute and the YMCA. Funding the two churchmen were Samuel Brooks and Richard Peacock, the embodiment of the values of moral and mental improvement. From modest backgrounds but equipped with a Grammar school education, both created engineering empires though invention, foresight and graft. They were the Bill Gates and Steve Jobs of their day, and to the young men of Gorton AFC they served as an example of what could be achieved through education and hard work.

Peacock and Brooks were also social engineers, and for them the Victoria Cross pattee would have had another meaning. Created during the Crimean War in 1856, the medal was the first to be awarded regardless of rank. It was the most prominent symbol of the sweeping reforms of the mid-Victorian period, which brought education and opportunity to working people. Historian Asa Briggs called it the "Age of Improvement", and many of the young men in the 1884-85 photograph were about to reap the benefits of the social mobility it offered. Great improvements in child literacy meant that, as boys, they would have found inspiration in the pages of popular weekly magazine, *Boys of England*. The magazine's tales of empire provided romantic role models, whose heroic exploits would have confirmed the belief once expressed by imperialist Cecil Rhodes that being born an Englishman was like winning a prize in a "lottery of life". Rhodes believed that "success in manly outdoor sports" such as football was essential for a prosperous life. The young Gorton men in the team photograph stood as testament to that. One of them, Walter Chew, would later become treasurer and a shareholder of the Manchester FA, while another, railway clerk Lawrence Furniss, rose from captain of a fledgling club to the glorious heights of chairman of Manchester City FC.

Pride in Battle

However, a close examination of the 1884-85 team photograph

leads to the most likely explanation of the Maltese Cross design. The shirts have varying necklines, irregularly-placed badges, and appear to be made of different materials, indicating that they were most likely sewn by the players' mothers (as most of their clothes would have been at that time). Furthermore, a striped pattern can clearly be seen on the arms and chest of Furniss's shirt, and possibly on the jersey of the player to his right. This suggests that the badges were sewn onto jerseys they already owned and may have worn whilst playing for previous clubs, including St Mark's. Other evidence points to the kits being home-made. Sports outfitters typically charged 3-4 shillings for football jerseys around this time, meaning that it would have cost £4 or more to fit out the club's two teams. However, Gorton AFC's annual accounts record a figure of just £1 16s 3d for "football requisites" that season.

The colour of the jerseys may have been shaped in part by practicality, as the kits would have been washed by the players' mothers each week. This probably ensured that dark colours were the norm for amateur clubs and whites rare. And in an era before away kits, the use of badge designs would have been an important way of distinguishing between the teams. In October 1877 a letter in the *Staffordshire Sentinel* complained about the lack of "distinctive uniforms" in association games. "It becomes impossible to follow the game properly unless you can readily distinguish the opposition players", its author wrote.

Another appeal of the design would have been its simplicity, requiring just four identical triangles. But most significantly, the cross pattee would have possessed an instantly recognisable meaning to the young men in the team photograph. In August 1884 – just two months before Gorton AFC was founded – a man named Carlisle was presented with a "gold centred Maltese Cross" after reaching the Irwell Hotel in Broughton to complete the 4,386th mile out of a 5,100 mile walk in 100 days. The award of the medal indicates that the Maltese Cross had been a symbol of Manchester sporting life for nearly two decades. It represented bravery, physical endurance and the dreams of self-improvement.

In short, a symbol of sporting glory.

A Manchester Sunday school centenary medal, 1880

A VC-shaped commemorative medal from 1894

A ginger beer bottle from the late Victorian period. A member of the family who owned Whitehead & Co, Edward Whitehead, was one of the defendants in the fancy dress ball trial in 1880, in which he was named as a 20-year-old "bottle maker", living on Oxford Road, Manchester.

CHAPTER 7

PROFESSIONALS, POLITICS, AND PINTS

On the day the formation of Gorton AFC was announced, 25 October 1884, a mass-meeting at Gorton's Liberal Club descended into violence after around 30 members of Gorton's Irish Land League disrupted it. After twice being forcibly ejected from the meeting the men, who had "the appearance of Irish labourers", returned a third time and a mass brawl erupted. The cause of the fracas was the Liberal government's policy on Ireland, a subject that dominated the General Election of November-December 1885.

For most Gortonions, continued battles over the Irish Problem meant that ethnicity and politics were inextricably linked. In this context the venue of Gorton AFC's first annual dinner on 20 April 1885, the Justice Birch Hotel on Hyde Road, is a significant one. The Hotel was the meeting place for Gorton's Conservative Association and Ashbury's Masonic Lodge, and was the home of Gorton Orange Lodge 202 from 1877 onward.

A newspaper report of the dinner named James Moores as the club's president and William Beastow as its vice-president. The pair were deeply involved in Conservative politics at this time and both had attended meetings of Gorton's Conservative Parliamentary Debating Society at the Justice Birch (Beastow was vice-chairman, and was supported by Moores).

A Political Football

The year 1885 was a crucial one in British politics. The number of eligible male voters almost doubled between 1880 and 1885 (the electorate increased from 2,338,809 in 1880 to 4,094,674 in 1885) while the Redistribution of Seats Act, which became law in June 1885, increased the number of MPs in urban areas at the expense of rural ones and created the Manchester

East constituency. A new working-class urban electorate was waiting to be won over, and football's unique pulling power would soon be used for political ends. According to P F Clarke's *Lancashire and the New Liberalism*, the use of local football clubs for electioneering had become common practise by the early 1900s. Indeed, correspondence between Ashton's Conservative MP Sir Max Aitken and his agent J C Buckley, dated July 1911 to May 1912, reveal the depth of the ties between sports clubs and political parties.

> "The Unitarian Sunday School F.C. was 'Liberal to a man'. Albion Young Men: 'No, you already subscribe to this lot through their Football club – they will work against you to a man next election.' Albion Choir F.C. 'No, these are all Radical lads, and will be against you.' Gatefield FC.: 'This is one of our own lot. I advise £1.1.0. St James's School: 'This is all right, a guinea will do a lot of good – they are a loyal lot.'"

Exactly when football became politicised is unclear, but by the 1888-89 season Conservative MPs Arthur Balfour and James Fergusson, and Liberal MP Charles Schwann, were vice-presidents of Newton Heath FC, while six days before the General Election of October 1891 Fergusson kicked off a match between Newton Heath and Ardwick.

Whether Moores and Beastow were putting Gorton AFC to political use at this time is unclear, particularly as there is no evidence the pair played an active role in organising the club's affairs (the club's accounts have a separate entry for income from honorary members, and their titles may have merely been the result of them paying a higher subscription than other club members). But Richard Peacock, whose £5 donation covered most of the club's expenses that season, was probably hoping for some political advantage. Peacock sought the Conservative party nomination around the time the club was formed but, in the 1885 General Election, won the Gorton seat as a Liberal (he initially wanted to stand as Conservative-Liberal).

Political tensions were certainly running high at this time. On 23 March 1885 a meeting of Gorton ratepayers was so "uproarious" (Beastow and two other Local Board members were hissed at by political opponents whilst giving their addresses) that chairman G H Underwood had threatened to call the police.

To Business

Gorton AFC's annual dinner, though, was a much more agreeable affair. The club's accounts suggest that 15 members received 6d complimentary tickets for the event. One of them, Frederick Hopkinson, performed a rendition of *The Old Brigade*, a popular march written in 1881 by Edward Slater (who also composed Danny Boy). W Chew (probably William due to his age and his position as Gorton's umpire) then led the singing of the naval march Hearts of Oak. That song was the Victorian equivalent of a terrace anthem, and its lyrics probably give a good insight into the mindset of the club's members that evening:

"Come, cheer up, my lads, 'tis to glory we steer,
To add something more to this wonderful year;
To honour we call you, as freemen not slaves,
For who are so free as the sons of the waves?

Heart of oak are our ships, jolly tars are our men,
We always are ready; steady, boys, steady!
We'll fight and we'll conquer again and again".

Reading the annual report, Hopkinson announced that considerable progress had been made that season. The club had 25 active members with a promise of a good increase the following season. Things had also gone well on the pitch, with the team finishing the season with a respectable record of P16 W7 D2 L7 F31 A21.

Unfortunately, it appears that Gorton AFC no longer had a

ground. The last recorded match at Pink Bank Lane had been on 24 January, and as the financial accounts for the following season included £2 compensation for "loss of ground" it's likely the club had been evicted mid-season. The reason for this is unclear. A 1905 map of the area shows what appears to be a cricket ground and pavilion on the western side of Pink Bank Lane, so this may have been the site of the Kirkmanshulme Cricket Ground, referred to in the *Book of Football*, that the club were evicted from after the cricketers became "very irate".

So that summer the club moved to land owned by the Bull's Head public house on Reddish Lane, which had already been the venue for sporting events such as shooting after former landlord William Riding became licensee in May 1880. The new ground was probably located on the 12 acres of "good grazing land" that new landlord Henry Jones had advertised to let in June 1885. The land was sandwiched between Reddish Lane and the Manchester and Ashton canal (the same canal beside which Manchester City's Ethiad Stadium now stands) and was close to Reddish station – the next stop down the MSLR / Midland Railway's Belle Vue line. The exact location of the pitch is not known, though it may have been located on what is now the playing field of the Aspinal Primary School.

It's also unclear why the club chose that location, particularly as it lay on the very eastern side of town, 1.5 miles from Pink Bank Lane and more than two miles from where most of the players lived. It's possible that there were no available sites in West Gorton following the club's eviction, though the easy availability of land south of Belle Vue gardens suggests this is unlikely. In 1880, for instance, a 15-acre plot on Pink Bank Lane was withdrawn from sale after attracting no bidders, while a four acre field was also available to let that year. Politics may also have been a factor in the move. The Bull's Head had been the headquarters of the local Orange Lodge since the 1830s, an organisation that played an active role in the General Election later that year.

More likely is that the Pink Bank Lane area was deemed unsuitable for an ambitious football club. Despite reasonable attendances that season (a match report noted a "fair number of spectators" for the home game on 22 November) the club's accounts reveal that only £1 1s 10d was taken in gate receipts. That's the equivalent of just 23 spectators per match paying 3d each, a typical admission charge at that time. It may be that problems enclosing the ground meant most spectators were watching for free. Admission charges at the Belle Vue gardens also did not help matters. Its sixpence entry fee on Saturdays doubled to one shilling for anyone admitted after 4pm, the time when football matches were still in full swing.

Although the Bull's Head was located in a much more sparsely-populated area than West Gorton, it was the only public house within a mile radius, and the only one close to the giant Reddish iron works. So the prospect of the pub's customers increasing gate receipts (they rose from £1 1s 10d to £2 5s 8d after the move) might have been a tempting one. At this time Gorton AFC were near the bottom of the country's football pyramid. The club had an average income of just 6s 10d per game in its first season and made a meagre profit of 2s 3d per game. To put its finances into perspective, that season's £10 9s income was almost 200 times less than that of Bolton Wanderers, who recorded a turnover of £1,949 in 1884-85. However, fresh opportunities were about to open up.

The Triumph of Working Class Football

On 20 July, after years of squabbling and threats, the Football Association finally lifted its ban on professionalism. Although merely acknowledging what was common practice among clubs outside London and the Home Counties – which by this time included payments of up to £5 per match for star players – the rule change heralded a fundamental shift in the game's development. According to Adrian Harvey's *Football: The First Hundred Years*, the resistance to professionalism by the public school-dominated southern clubs was shaped by the dislike of its working-class nature. And once the floodgates of professionalism had been opened it wasn't long before the southern clubs with public school origins jumped ship. The changing nature of football is probably best illustrated by the make-up of clubs in the FA Challenge Cup. Once the sole preserve of well-educated gentlemen, by the end of the 1880s 29 of the 32 clubs in its first round had working-class origins. According to Harvey, as interest in football waned among the upper classes, rugby, "a game as yet unaffected by extensive working-class participation, increased in popularity among the old boys."

The era of football as the sport of the working man had officially begun. "On every vacant piece of land can be seen the schoolboy and operative giving an exposition of its rules," the *Preston Guardian* wrote on 27 August 1884. According to the 5 January 1885 edition of *The Athlete*,

> "Never in the memory of man... has any game
> attained such a wonderful popularity, and the public
> interest, instead of waning, grows stronger year by
> year."

Huge attendances were now being reported at games. In March 1882 a Darwen v Blackburn Rovers match had attracted close to 20,000 paying spectators, while in the 1883-84 season crowds of 15,000-plus were recorded at football matches in Bolton, Nottingham and Derby. In Manchester, though, attendances were much lower. The final of the inaugural Manchester Cup in April 1885 – in which Hurst defeat Newton Heath 3-0 – was watched by only 3,500 spectators, while the biggest reported crowd for a match in Gorton was just 1,000. However, with the city's population now around 400,000 the potential for growth for Manchester's fledgling clubs was enormous. Manchester football also stood to benefit from a new FA rule which required professional players to have lived within six miles of a club's headquarters for at least two years. While clubs from Lancashire mill towns now had to restrict the search for new talent to their limited local populations, Manchester clubs could now benefit from having a huge well of aspiring footballers from which to draw. In fact, with enough ambition, a Manchester club could even grow mightier than the great Blackburn Rovers.

Gorton AFC's accounts 1884-85

Income	£	s	d
R. Peacock, Esq.	5	0	0
Members subscriptions	3	2	4
Hon. members subscriptions	1	5	0
Gate money	1	1	10
Total	10	9	2
Expenditure			
Rent of ground	3	0	0
Rent of dressing room		15	0
Football requisites	1	16	3
Stationary, printing, postages	1	17	3
Umpire expenses		14	
Subscriptions to M & D Association		10	6
Comp. tickets for dinner		7	6
Total	**9**	**0**	**6**

The Club That Turned to Drink

Many of the Gorton AFC players had learned football under the guidance of the clergy and social reformers. As the goal was to instill a "Muscular" Christianity in young men, attracting spectators was not a concern. Match reports during those first few years were merely a record of events, praising the hard work and skill of individual players, and the good conduct of teams. But the introduction of profit into the game brought about a new set of priorities, one that began to be reflected in newspaper coverage. Following Gorton's 5-0 win at home to Manchester Clifford on 10 January 1885, the local newspaper stated

> "The Gorton Association Football Club, newly
> formed this season, have taken all before them.
> They beat a strong team of the Manchester Clifford
> on Saturday by five goals to nil. They have really
> only lost one match this season, and that was with
> only half their team at Tottingham Park. This is
> good form, and the success of the club has caused
> whispers that it would not be very surprising to hear
> of them bringing the Manchester and District
> Challenge Cup to Gorton."

To place Gorton AFC's chances above the more established – and more successful – clubs such as Manchester AFC, Hurst and Newton Heath was somewhat optimistic. In fact, this may be the first example of media hype involving a Gorton football club. But then, Mancunians throughout time have proved to be very successful at "bigging it up". An art exhibition created by the city in 1857 – in which 1.3 million visitors viewed 16,000 works of art – is believed to this day to be the largest exhibition of its kind the world has ever held. And in typically Manchester fashion it also made a lot of money, including a £50,000 profit for the train companies. As contemporary chronicler Edward Parry wrote: "The first idea of Manchester is business, and the second idea of Manchester is business, and the seventy times seventh idea of Manchester is business".

Football's money-making potential would certainly have not escaped the notice of the educated and ambitious young men of Gorton AFC. Indeed, professionalism was even encouraged by Manchester evangelicals such as William Warburton, who argued in August 1884 that it would raise standards and improve the game's popularity. However, the move to the Bull's Head also marks the crossing of a cultural divide. Gorton AFC were about to become entwined with another strand of football's DNA: the club that served to entertain pub customers. This form of football would undoubtedly have been met with disapproval by the likes of Warburton, Connell and Brooks.

Alcohol use was an important issue to many connected to St Mark's. Arthur Connell was an active member of the Church of England Temperance Society and chaired West Gorton's monthly Band of Hope temperance meetings. Samuel Brooks snr, one of the dignitaries on the Gorton team photo and a donor to St Mark's, was also a firm advocate of temperance. On 11 September 1880 he told his assembled workers at Union Iron's 21st anniversary dinner,

> "I would also point out to you the benefit of using
> your spare time and holiday times in a rational way;
> not in wasting your energies and robbing your
> wives and families by drinking".

His comments are a good example of the battle fought by the Church and business owners over male leisure time – one that the Church was losing. Manchester's brewing money had already softened opposition to alcohol. Indeed, in December 1878, Alfred Stopford, a brewer and member of Gorton's Board of Health, donated £100 towards the £400 cost of enlargements to St Mark's school. By 1885 Arthur Connell had effectively waved the white flag of surrender when he campaigned on behalf of brewer Daniel Flattely, the Conservative candidate who lost to Richard Peacock in the General Election that December.

Now Gorton AFC's fortunes were about to become intertwined

with the brewing industry's. And in 1880s Manchester, the fortunes of its brewers were bound up with the Conservative cause. On 21 April 1886 Beastow and Moores attended the fourth annual soiree of the Gorton Conservatives at Belle Vue. Also present that night was Stephen Chesters Thompson, managing director of Chester's Brewery in Ardwick and election agent for future prime minister Arthur Balfour.

A year earlier, the larger-than-life Chesters Thompson had masterminded Balfour's election victory as MP for East Manchester. After Gorton AFC moved to Hyde Road, Ardwick in 1887 – and adopted the district's name – Chesters Thompson set about turning Ardwick AFC into a nationwide force. In 1890 he spent £600 to £700 of the brewery's money on new players, three times the club's annual income and the equivalent of £700 million today. By 1893 Chesters Thompson had lavished £2,600 of company money on the club. Unfortunately, he hadn't told the brewery's shareholders, who had been footing the bill for that, and his many other spending sprees. Chesters Thompson was sacked, put on trial for fraud and forced into bankruptcy. In 1894 Ardwick AFC also perished, but following its demise, the club was reincarnated once more – this time into its final form as Manchester City Football Club.

Anna Connell and All That

Big football clubs thrive on mythology, particularly when it confers exclusivity. Since the 1980s Manchester City FC has had its own unique tale, one immortalised in a broadcast by BBC Radio Four's *Woman's Hour* in 2007. It claimed that City was the only major club founded by a woman, a vicar's daughter named Anna Connell. Her motivation, we were told, was to save local young men from social deprivation and gang-fighting.

Broadsheet sports journalists loved the story. After the club was taken over that summer by a deposed Thai prime minister with a questionable human rights record, some lamented City's fall from grace from its original aims of fighting for social justice. The club's marketing department also embraced the story, and expanded it to include Anna's family. In the summer of 2012 the club revamped one of the hospitality suites at the Ethiad Stadium, renaming it the Connell Club. It was a place the Rev. Connell would have despised, where sensual pleasures are pampered to, alcohol served on arrival and gambling encouraged. In fact, the Connell Club was the most wonderfully inappropriate use of a club legend since a bar at Maine Road was named after lifelong teetotaler Billy Meredith.

But the Connells' place in City's history was only temporary. Since the first edition of this book in May 2013, references to the family have been removed from the club's official website, and the Connell Club was quietly renamed the Chairman's Club. However, amid the confusion a new picture of City's origins is emerging. While it is not as newsworthy as the story of the "Vicar's daughter", it is one that has relevance to all eras.

It is a story of a football club created by ambitious, educated young working men. This new arrival to club football was a minnow compared to the giants from surrounding cities. At the end of their first season they had no ground, meagre support and only £1 8s 8d in the bank. But its founders were steeped in a spirit of enterprise that had been moulded by Manchester's engineering visionaries, and set about constructing a giant.

Two decades later the club had lifted the FA Cup and by the 1930s it had become one of the biggest football clubs in the world. Indeed, in 1934 City attracted a gate of 84,569 – to this day the largest home crowd that has ever been seen at an English football match.

Manchester City's descent into becoming football's most famous under-achievers took as long as the rise, spanning four decades from the late 1970s. It was a decline that would have been unthinkable to pre-WW2 City fans, as much as the idea of Manchester United being relegated would be to their fans today. But City's long malaise came to an abrupt end in 2008 when the club was bought by one of the world's richest men, Emirati petro-billionaire Sheikh Mansour bin Zayed Al Nahyan. By 2013 the problems resulting from decades of underinvestment had been solved with a cash injection of around £500million, and Manchester City FC had regained its place among football's world elite.

A Man's World

Today's club would be an alien place to its Victorian founders; owned by a man they would have called a "Mohammedan", managed by a Chilean Roman Catholic and with a playing squad made up of the world's colours and creeds. The brand of football played by today's teams would be equally alien. Whilst no doubt marvelling at the circus skills of some modern-day players, the diving and feigning of injury would be viewed with contempt. After all, manbags filled with skin-care products and deodorants had no place in the life of a late 19th-century Englishman. This calloused masculinity was constructed through strength and bravery. A man had to be prepared for his role as head of the household, with a duty to protect – and make decisions for – those whom he believed God had made weaker: his wife and children (and legally they were only *his* children). So where better to learn those qualities than the football field, with the constant danger of serious injury and occasionally death? Newspapers talked of the "Manly game of football", including how Leeds Football Club was created for the "encouragement of manly sports". As the *Manchester Courier* declared in February 1881:

> "To be a good football player, a young man must
> take care of himself, must accustom himself to bear
> severe strain, to run and to kick freely. He must
> control his appetite, practice self-denial, and
> cultivate manliness in all its characteristics".

It certainly wasn't a pastime for women to engage in, as twenty-two aspiring female footballers learned that year. On Monday 20 June 1881 a "ladies' football match" took place at the ground of Cheetham Football Club, in Tetlow Fold, Cheetham. A "large number of spectators" had assembled to watch "eleven of England and eleven of Scotland". According to the *Manchester Evening News* after 30 minutes play the pitch was invaded "and the wildest confusion prevailed, the players having to make good their escape". The following day another big crowd assembled for a second match at Cheetham. Although extra precautions had been taken to secure order, the *Courier* reported that after several attempts by the crowd to take possession of the ground "a great rush was made by those occupying the higher land and the football ground was speedily taken possession of". Again, the female players were pelted with missiles, but with the help of a number of police constables they made it to the safety of a wagonette pulled by four horses.

The hostility was also voiced in the newspapers. The secretary of Cheetham FC, Edwin Smales, wrote to the *Courier* to assure readers that his club played no part in arranging the games, a word he placed in inverted commas. The Rev. May Lund of St John's Anglican church in Cheetham also wrote to deplore the event. While condemning the violence, Lund also noted that it was "regarded in many quarters as a fine exhibition of a manly sense of righteous indignation against an unbecoming show". Nor was the violence at Cheetham an isolated incident. Five weeks earlier the women had been forced to abandon a game in Glasgow after the majority of the 5,000 crowd stormed the field, "roughly jostled" them and pelted them with wooden stakes.

Determining the root cause of violent acts is never an easy task, but the most likely explanation for the anger appears to be that it was the product of the rigid gender roles of late Victorian Britain. Religious reformers took a particular interest in defining those roles. In their eyes the whole point of football was to expunge undesirable feminine qualities in men – the "poison of effeminacy" as "Muscular" Christianity's pioneer Charles Kingsley called it. According to J A Mangan and James Walvin's *Manliness and Morality*, the feminine ideal demanded "docility, commitment to domesticity and subservience". Not only was it undesirable for women to seek the masculine traits of strength and bravery, but the playing of football by women would call into question the manly nature of the sport itself.

Just as the Manchester transvestite ball in 1880 had posed a threat to the ideal of masculinity, so too did the playing of football by women "habited as men". But with the women's rights movement still in its infancy, the matches at Cheetham represented a premature attempt to storm a bastion of manliness.

For its Victorian founders, football was unquestionably a man's game.

List of Appendices

Appendix 1: Location of grounds

1. Site of Longsight cricket ground, home of Longsight Cricket Club until 1891.

2. Jennison's field, probable location of St Mark's matches, 1880-83.

3. Land near Union Iron works, probable first ground for West Gorton Association, 1882-83.

4. Common land off Queen's Road (also called Clemington Park), probable home of Belle Vue Rangers, 1882-83, and home of West Gorton, 1883-84.

5. Pink Bank Lane, home of Gorton Association, 1884-85 (& likely location of Kirkmanshulme Cricket Ground).

6. Ground beside Bull's Head Inn, home of Gorton AFC, 1885-87, & Gorton Villa, 1887.

7. Site of Hyde Road ground, home of Ardwick AFC, 1887-94, & Manchester City FC, 1894-1923.

8. Site of Bank Street stadium, home of Newton Heath / Manchester United FC, 1893-1910.

9. Location for City stadium proposed in 1914 (and possibly in 1902-03).

10. Etihad Stadium, home of Manchester City FC, 2003 to present.

Appendix 2: The first association games involving Manchester clubs

Season 1875-76 to 1877-78 (away games shaded)

Date	Team	Team	Venue	Res
13 Nov 1875	Mr. J. Nall's team (Manchester Association)	Mr T G Smith's team (Manchester Association)	Moss Side (Land adjoining Pepperhill Farm)	0-1
11 Mar 1876	Broughton Wasps	Manchester Association	Lower Broughton	1-0
16 Dec 1876	Manchester Association	Sheffield	Longsight Cricket Club	0-4
10 Feb 1877	Manchester Association	Stoke	Eccles	1-2
24 Feb 1877	Sheffield	Manchester Association	Bramall Lane (Sheffield Rules)	14-0
20 Oct 1877	Broughton Wasps	Manchester Association	Lower Broughton	1-1
27 Oct 1877	Derby Grammar School	Manchester Association	Derby	7-0
3 Nov 1877	Manchester Association	Darwen	Eccles (FA Cup tie)	1-3
1 Dec 1877	Manchester Association	Darwen	Eccles	0-2
15 Dec 1877	Nottingham	Manchester Association	Nottingham	6-0
26 Jan 1878	Manchester Association	Stoke	Longsight Cricket Club	0-2
9 Feb 1878	Manchester Association	Nottinghamshire	Longsight Cricket Club	1-4

1878-79 season (away games shaded)

Date	Team	Team	Venue	Res
2 Nov 1878	Manchester Wanderers	Stoke	Whalley Range "small number of spectators"	1-4
11 Nov 1878	Stoke	Manchester Wanderers	Stoke (under floodlights)	1-1
13 Nov 1878	Stoke	Manchester Wanderers	Stoke (under floodlights)	3-3
8 Feb 1879	Manchester Wanderers	Eagley	Probably Whalley Range	0-2
15 Feb 1879	Sheffield	Manchester Wanderers	Bramall Lane Sheffield	3-1
22 Mar 1879	Manchester Wanderers	Sheffield	Whalley Range "200 spectators"	0-1
29 Mar 1879	Manchester Wanderers	Macclesfield	Whalley Range (return match)	2-1
5 April 1879	Manchester Wanderers	Derby Grammar School 2nd XI	Probably Whalley Range	3-2
26 Apr 1879	Birch 2nd	Cheetham 1st	Whalley Range	2-1
26 Apr 1879	Birch 1st	Cheetham 2nd	Whalley Range	2-0
26 Apr 1879	Birch 2nd	Birch 1st	Whalley Range	3-1
26 Apr 1879	Broughton Rangers	Birch 2nd	Whalley Range	2-1

Appendix 3: Match details for 1880-81 season

St Mark's first recorded line-up, 13 November 1880

layer	Age	Occupation	Address	Notes
John Beastow	18	Engine fitter	178 Clowes St	Son of William Beastow
William Sumner (captain)	19	Engineering student	Lodger at 122 Clowes St	
Frederick Hopkinson	18	Clerk	71 Clowes St	Chorister & CC secretary
William Chew or Walter Chew	18 15	Warehouse clerk "	12 Elizabeth St "	
Henry Heggs	20	Mechanic fitter	6 Hampton St, Ardwick	Father baker & flour dealer
William Downing	19	Clerk	47 Elizabeth St	Born Bramhall
Richard Hopkinson	20	Clerk	71 Clowes St	Chorister
Edward Kitchen	18	Clerk (prob. insurance)	4 Tank Row	Baptised at St Mark's
Arthur McDonald	15	Grinder	25 Robinson St	b N Ireland
John Pilkington	18		137 Hyde Rd	Father baker & flour dealer
Charles Beastow	18	Clerk in iron works	178 Clowes St	Step-son of W Beastow
James Collinge	18	Warehouse man	Lodged at 25 Boundary St.	

St Mark's fixtures 1880-81

Date	Opponents	Venue	Res	Notes
13 Nov 1880	Baptist (Macclesfield)	Longsight, near Belle Vue (probably Jennison's field)	L 2-1	12-a-side "very pleasant" game Umpires E Hardy, A Houghton
27 Nov 1880	Manchester Arcadians	Longsight	0-0	Opponents had cotton warehouse and Sunday school connection
18 Dec 1880	Hurst	Ashton-under-Lyne	L 3-0	Opponents probably cotton mill team
31 Dec 1880	Broadbottom	Broadbottom	L 3-0	Opponents probably cotton mill team St Mark's 9 men "very pleasant game"
8 Jan 1881	Manchester Arcadians	Moston Lane, Harpurhey	0-0	
22 Jan 1881	Baptist Rovers	London Road, Macclesfield	L 4-0	"Pleasant though rather one sided game"
26 Feb 1881	Hurst	Longsight	L 7-0	Ground "in a very sloppy state"
5 Mar 1881	Manchester Wanderers Reserves	Brook's Bar	1-1	St Mark's 9 men 60min play
12 Mar 1881	Stalybridge Clarence	Tame Valley (played before "good number of spectators")	L 5-0	Opponents probably cotton mill team with C of E links "Friendly game "
9 Mar 1881	Stalybridge Clarence	Tame Valley	W 3-1	Stalybridge XI included captain of Broadbottom

First recorded appearances, 26 Feb 1881

New player	Age	Occupation	Address	Notes
Albert Keates	17	Clerk (book-keeper in 1886)	84 Clowes St (lived with with uncle)	Played for St Mark's Juniors
Edward Groves	17	Warehouse man	Ardwick	
Joseph Smith	24	Locomotive fitter	Lodger at 89 Birch St	
Harroway				

Appendix 4: the growth of football in the Manchester area

Year	Number of clubs
1875-76	1
1876-77	1
1877-78	3
1878-79	2
1879-80	3
1880-81	7
1881-82	14
1882-83	21
1883-84	29

Appendix 5: *1881-82 season*

St Mark's fixtures 1881-82

Date	Opponents	Venue	Res	Notes
15 Oct 1881	Bentfield	Greenfield	L 1-0	Opponents probably cotton mill side
29 Oct 1881	Hurst Clarence	Longsight	L 3-0	"Good number of spectators" "Friendly" & "most pleasant" game
12 Nov 1881	Newton Heath	Newton Heath	L 3-0	"Pleasant game"
19 Nov 1881	Manchester Arcadians	Harpurhey	W 1-0	
3 Dec 1881	Bentfield	Longsight	W 3-2	
31 Dec 1881	Broadbottom	Broadbottom	L 3-0	Umpire Mr Osborne W Gorton 9 players "very pleasant game"
7 Jan 1882	Manchester Arcadians	Longsight	1-1	Umpire Mr Osborne Ground in "heavy state"
14 Jan 1882	Haughton Dale	Longsight	W 8-1	Opponents probably wireworks team (owner C of E benefactor)
28 Jan 1882	Hurst	Ashton-under-Lyne	L 6-0	
25 Feb 1882	Broadbottom	Longsight	W 3-0	
4 Mar 1882	Newton Heath (L & YR)	Longsight	W 2-1	Umpire Mr Osborne NH "Railwaymen" a man short "Loud cheers" for goal
11 Mar 1882	Haughton Dale	Haughton Dale	L 1-0	Umpires Osborne, James Walton

First recorded appearances, 15 October 1881

New player	Age	Occupation	Address	Notes
John Bottomley	18	Machine works apprentice	48 Clowes St	Born Bradford, Lancashire
H Hanson				
Joseph Clegg	24	Clogger	74 Thomas St	

29 October

R Millard				

12 November

Perver				

19 November

Isaac Bower	23	Joiner	251 Hyde Rd	Played for St Mark's

3 December

New player	Age	Occupation	Address	
James Taylor or Samuel Taylor	23 18	Lifter in carriage works Wagon maker (Unemployed)	5 Railway View 257 Thomas St	
McKenna				
Charles Roberts or James Roberts	17 19	Labourer	98 Taylor St 98 Taylor St	b. S Africa b. S Africa

31 December

Joseph Anderson	27	Engine fitter	27 Woodhouse St	

5 February 1882

Edward Holt	26	Loco engine fitter	8 Booth St	Married
or Charles Holt	26	draper	129 Clowes St	Married

Belle Vue Rangers fixtures 1881-82

Date	Opponents	Venue	Res	Notes
14 Jan 1882	Hurst Park Road	Ashton-under-Lyne	L 4-1	"Easy victory" Belle Vue 10 men
18 Jan 1882	Hurst Park Road Reserves	West Gorton	1-1	"Very even game"

First recorded appearances, 14 January 1882

Player	Age	Occupation	Address	Notes
Joseph Payton	20	Screw bolt maker	17 Brougham St	Moved from Dudley 1865-73
Hitchen				
Edward Bower	21		251 Hyde Road	Brother of Isaac Bower
D Donohue				
Patterson	26		2 Leigh Place	
Patterson	23		2 Leigh Place	
P Donohue				
W Russell				
Joseph Hickson	18	Engine fitters apprentice	18 Elizabeth St	Family lived in India & Ireland
Walter Chew (captain)	17	Warehouse clerk	12 Elizabeth St	

First recorded appearances, 28 January

Player	Age	Occupation	Address	Notes
Avery				
Harry Wathey	15	Spindle turner	3 Hoylake St Openshaw	
McCabe	20	Card grinder	15 Dawson St	

Appendix 6:1882-83 season

St Mark's fixtures 1882-83

Date	Opponents	Venue	Res	Notes
14 Oct 1882	Haughton Dale	Haughton Green	0-0	
28 Oct 1882	Bentfield	West Gorton	L 2-0	St Mark's 10 men
4 Nov 1882	Hurst Clarence A	Ashton-under Lyne	2-2	St Mark's 8 men. Belle Vue Rangers play same day
18 Nov 1882	Hurst	Ashton-under Lyne	L 6-0	St Mark's 10 men
25 Nov 1882	Manchester Association	Gorton	L 1-0	Belle Vue Rangers play at home same day
2 Dec 1882	Marple	Marple	1-1	St Mark's 10 men. Opponents probably cotton mill team
6 Jan 1883	Marple	Belle Vue	L 4-2	
3 Feb 1883	Broadbottom	Broadbottom	L 2-0	
17 Feb 1883	Bentfield	Greenfield	L 7-0	

First recorded appearances, 4 November 1882

Player	Age	Occupation	Address	Notes
Nichol				
C R Sumner				Probably brother of William Sumner

25 November

Johnson				

2 December

Carrick				

3 February 1883

New Player	Age	Occupation	Address	Notes
Ashworth				
Michael Clark	18	Iron moulder	46 & 48 Gorton Brook St	Born Manchester Father b. Sligo, Ireland
John Fletcher	26	Warehouse man	73 Morton St	Born Gloucester Married
Thomas Sykes	21	Iron fitter	65 Wellington St Barber Shop	Born Gorton

17 February

New Player	Age	Occupation	Address	Notes
Thomas Whitelegg	18	Newspaper clerk	175 Hyde Rd	Mother tobacconist

West Gorton Association fixtures 1882-83

Evidence about West Gorton Association's origins is sketchy, but it appears that the club's first recorded fixture was on 6 January 1883, when it was listed as "West Gorton (a team)" in newspaper reports.

Date	Opponents	Venue	Res	Notes
Jan 6 1883	Greenheys	Whalley Range (home of Manchester Association)	1-1	West Gorton 9 men (played 10 a side) Opponents formed October 1882 by Presbyterian Church
Feb 24 1883	Middleton	Gorton (possibly beside Union Iron works)	W 1-0	West Gorton 9 men "Neither side fully represented

West Gorton Association first recorded line-up, 24 Feb

Player	Age	Occupation	Address	Notes
Nichol				Played for St Mark's
W Chew (captain)	17	Warehouse clerk	12 Elizabeth St	Captained Belle Vue Rangers & played for St Mark's
Kitchen	20	Clerk (prob. insurance)	4 Tank Row	Played for St Mark's
Michael Clark	18	Iron moulder	46 & 48 Gorton Brook St	Born Manchester Father b. Sligo, Ireland
Millard				
Joseph Anderson	28	Engine fitter	27 Woodhouse St	Played for St Mark's
Clegg				
William Patterson (1)	23	Clerk	2 Leigh Place	Scottish parents Played for Belle Vue Rangers

(1) Could also be 26-year-old engine tenter James Patterson

Belle Vue Rangers fixtures 1882-83

Date	Opponents	Venue	Res	Notes
21 Oct 1882	Hurst Park Rd Reserves	West Gorton	W 6-0	
4 Nov 1882	Endon Reserves	Bollington	W 5-4	"Very unpleasant game"
18 Nov 1882	Macclesfield Wanderers	West Gorton	L 5-2	
6 Jan 1883	Hurst Park Rd Reserves	Ashton-under-Lyne	L 3-1	
20 Jan 1883	Hurst Clarence Reserves	Ashton-under-Lyne	W 3-1	
27 Jan 1883	Macclesfield Wanderers	Macclesfield	1-1	"Wanderers played a rough game"
10 Mar 1883	Hurst Clarence Reserves	Ashton-under-Lyne	L 3-2	
17 Mar 1883	Denton	West Gorton	W 2-0	
31 Mar 1883	Stalybridge	Stalybridge	L 1-0	

Belle Vue Rangers
First recorded appearances, 21 October 1882

Player	Age	Occupation	Address	Notes
R Howarth				
Joseph Poole	27	Joiner	111 Victoria St	
John Fletcher	26	Warehouseman	73 Morton St	Born Gloucester Married
T Coffey				
T Allen				

First recorded appearances, 20 January 1883

Player	Age	Occupation	Address	Notes
E Hunt				
Edward Groves	19	Warehouseman	Ardwick	

First recorded appearances, 27 January

Player	Age	Occupation	Address	Notes
J Bowers				
Edward Kitchen	22	Clerk	4 Tank Row	

First recorded appearance, 17 March

S Vale				

St Mark's recorded line-ups 1882-83

14 Oct (A) Haughton Dale 0-0	4 Nov (A) Hurst Clarence 2-2	25 Nov (H) Manchester Association L 1-0	2 Dec (A) Marple 1-1
11 men	**8 men**	**11 men**	**10 men**
C Beastow			C Beastow
Pilkington		Pilkington	
Bower			Bower
F Hopkinson			F Hopkinson
Kitchen	Kitchen	Kitchen	Kitchen
Groves	Groves	Groves	Groves
Anderson	Anderson	Anderson	
Macdonald			Macdonald
W Chew	W Chew	W Chew	W Chew
Clegg			
W H Chew			
	Taylor	Taylor	
	C R Sumner	C R Sumner	
	Sumner (captain)	Sumner (captain)	Sumner (captain)
	Nichol		
		Downing	
		R Hopkinson	
		Johnson	Johnson
			Caddick

Line-ups of all clubs, January to February 1883

Belle Vue	St Mark's	West Gorton	W Gorton AFC
27 Jan (A) v Macclesfield Wanderers	3 Feb (A) v Broadbottom	17 Feb (A) v Bentfield	24 Feb (H) v Middleton
1-1	L 2-0	L 7-0	W 1-0
11 men	9 men	9 men	8 men
	Ashworth		
Fletcher	Fletcher **BV**		
	Sykes		
	F Hopkinson **SM**		
	Nichol **SM**	Nichol	Nichol
W Chew (captain)	W Chew **SM** (captain)	W Chew (captain)	W Chew (captain)
Kitchen	Kitchen **SM BV**	Kitchen	Kitchen
Groves	Groves **SM**		
	Clark	Clark	Clark
Payton		Whitelegg	
Bower		Millard	Millard
Wathey		Anderson	Anderson
Bowers		Clegg **SM**	Clegg
Coffey		W H Chew **SM**	
Allen			Patterson **BV**

BV: also played for Belle Vue Rangers
SM: started season for St Mark's

Appendix 7: 1883-84 season

West Gorton fixtures, 1883-84

Date	Opponents	Venue	Res	Notes
6 Oct 1883	Hurdsfield (Macclesfield)	Queens Rd	W 4-3	
13 Oct 1883	Furness Vale	Queens Rd	W 1-0	1,000 spectators
20 Oct 1883	Manchester Arcadians	Queens Rd	W 2-0	About 100 spectators
3 Nov 1883	Broadbottom	Queens Rd	W 4-0	
17 Nov 1883	Pendleton Olympic	Pendleton	W 7-1	
24 Nov 1883	Marple	Marple	W 5-1	
1 Dec 1883	Bentfield	Greenfield	L 2-1	
8 Dec 1883	Furness Vale	Furness Vale	0-0	
22 Dec 1883	Haughton Dale	Haughton	W 4-1	
12 Jan 1884	Levenshulme	Queens Rd	2-2	
2 Feb 1884	Bentfield (Greenfield)	Queens Rd	W 2-1	600 spectators
9 Feb 1884	Broadbottom	Broadbottom	W 5-0	
16 Feb 1884	Greenheys	Greenheys	W 5-1	
15 Mar 1884	Haughton Dale	Haughton	L 1-0	
22 Mar 1884	Gorton Villa	Queens Rd	W 7-0	Game resulted in death of player
6 Apr 1884	Levenshulme	Levenshulme	1-1	

Appendix 8: 1884-85 season

Gorton Association fixtures 1884-85

Date	Opponents	Venue	Res	Notes
15 Nov 1884	Gorton Villa	Pink Bank La	W 4-1	
22 Nov 1884	Heywood St James	Pink Bank La	0-0	"Fair number of spectators"
6 Dec 1884	Manchester Clifford	Old Trafford	W 4-0	"Played in a very friendly manner"
13 Dec 1884	Heywood St James	Heywood	0-0	"Gorton did not arrive until after 4pm...In the second half, the play was in almost total darkness"
3 Jan 1885	Tottington	Tottington	L 3-0	
10 Jan 1885	Manc Clifford	Pink Bank La	W 3-0	
17 Jan 1885	Newton Heath	Pink Bank La	L 2-1	
24 Jan 1885	Manchester Clifford	Pink Bank La	W 3-0	Ground "very much against good play"
31 Jan 1885	Dalton Hall	Maine Road	L 1-0	"Large attendance of spectators"
14 Feb 1885	Gorton Villa	Ground of Gorton Villa	1-1	"Large number of spectators"
21 Feb 1885	Newton Heath	Newton Heath	L 6-0	"Fair number of spectators"

Gorton AFC first recorded line-up, 22 November 1884

Name	Age	Occupation	Address
Joseph Payton	20	Screw bolt maker	17 Brougham Street
Edward Bower	21		251 Hyde Road
Frederick Hopkinson	21	Clerk	71 Clowes Street
Lawrence Prenty	23	Railway porter	
Avery			
Edward Kitchen	22	Clerk	4 Tank Row, Longsight
W Turner (captain)		Student	
John Owen (1)	23	Locomotive engine fitter	26 Wellington Street, East Gorton
Walter Chew	19	Warehouse clerk	12 Elizabeth Street, West Gorton
J Booth (2)			
John Mellor (3)	20	Fitter	6 Peter Street, West Gorton

Occupations as listed in 1881 census (except Turner)

(1) Could also be George Owen, a 19-year-old publican's son living at 240, Upper Morton Street, Longsight.

(2) Could be John Thomas Booth, 19, an apprentice mechanic living at 36 Cross Lane; James Booth, 20, an apprentice living at 6 Mary St; or Joseph Booth, 25, an "Engine Smith Cotton Weaver" living at 20 Hope St.

(3) Could also be John James Mellor, 17, an iron driller living at 8, James Street, Gorton.

First recorded appearances, 6 December 1884

New Player	Age	Occupation	Address	Notes
Kenneth McKenzie	17		Probably b. Liverpool	Replaced Turner as captain
Jenkins				
Edward Groves	21	Warehouseman	50 Gorton St, Ardwick	Manchester born with Welsh mother
Lawrence Furniss	26	Probably railway clerk	Born Cromford	Former Cromford FC and CC captain
Thomas Kirk	22	Velvet buyer's assistant	18, Gorton Lane	Manchester born

First recorded appearances, 13 December 1884

New Player	Age	Occupation	Address	Notes
Isaac Bower	26	Joiner	251 Hyde Rd	Brother of Edward
D Strandring				
James E Aspinall	20	Iron moulder		Born Westhoughton
Bowden				
Ackroyd				

First recorded appearances, 3 January 1885

New Player	Age	Occupation	Address	Notes
Earnshaw				
Baker				
Samuel H Brooks	21	Son of Union Iron works owner	Slade House, Levenshulme	
John Fletcher	26	Warehouseman	73 Morton St	Born Gloucester Married

First recorded appearances, 17 January 1885

D Melville				
J Bain				
Mearns				

Appendix 9: Newton Heath fixtures

1880-81 (P5 W1 D1 L3 F2 A13)

Date	Opponents	Venue	Res
20 Nov 1880	Bolton Wanderers XI	Bolton	L 6-0
4 Dec	Manchester Arcadians	Harpurhey	0-0
22 Jan 1881	Bolton Wanderers XI	North Road	L 6-0
5 Feb	Bootle Reserves	North Road	W 2-0
15 Feb	Hurst	North Road	L 1-0

1881-82 (P8 W5 D1 L2 F17 A8)

Date	Opponents	Venue	Res
15 Oct 1881	Manchester Arcadians	North Road	W 3-0
22 Oct	Blackburn Olympic XI	Blackburn	L 4-0
12 Nov	St Mark's (West Gorton)	North Road	W 3-0
21 Jan 1882	Haughton Green	North Road	W 4-0
28 Jan	Haughton Green	Haughton Green	1-1
4 Mar	Southport	Southport	L 2-1
11 Mar	St Mark's (West Gorton)	Longsight	W 2-1
18 Mar	Manchester Arcadians	Harpurhey	W 3-0

Newton Heath 1882-83 (P8 W3 D2 L3 F19 A19)

Date	Opponents	Venue	Res
4 Nov 1882	Manchester Arcadians	North Road	W 4-0
18 Nov	Crewe Alexandra	Crewe	L 7-2
25 Nov	Bentfield	North Road	W 3-1
2 Dec	Middleton	North Road	W 4-3
13 Jan 1883	Astley Bridge Res	North Road	1-1
20 Jan	Bentfield	Greenfield	L 4-2
10 Feb	Manchester Arcadians	Harpurhey	0-0
17 Feb	Crewe Alexandra	North Road	L 3-0

Newton Heath 1883-84 (P18 W8 D5 L5 F33 A32)

Date	Opponents	Venue	Res
6 Oct 1883	Astley Bridge A	North Road	L 1-0
13 Oct	Haughton Dale	North Road	2-2
20 Oct	St Helen's	St Helen's	W 3-2
27 Oct	Blackburn Olympic Res	North Road	L 7-2
1 Dec	Manchester Arcadians	North Road	W 4-0
8 Dec	Earlestown	Earlestown	L 8-0
5 Jan 1884	Bootle Wanderers	North Road	W 6-0
12 Jan	Bentfield	Greenfield	1-1
19 Jan	St Helen's	North Road	W 3-1
26 Jan	Haughton Dale	Haughton Dale	W 1-0
30 Jan	St Helens	North Road	W 3-1
2 Feb	Greenheys	North Road	W 1-0
9 Feb	Bootle Wanderers	Bootle	1-1
23 Feb	Blackburn Olympic XI	North Road	0-0
1 Mar	Hurst Brook Olympic	Ashton-under- Lyne	L 3-1
8 Mar	Manchester Arcadians	Harpurhey	W 4-0
15 Mar	Astley Bridge Res	Astley Bridge	0-0
25 Mar	Greenheys	Greenheys	L 5-1

Newton Heath 1884-85 (P28 W21 D3 L4 F85 A35)

Date	Comp	Opponents	Att	Venue	Res
20 Sep	LC Rd1	Haydock Temperance		North Road	W 4-0
4 Oct		Earlestown Res		North Road	W 2-1
11 Oct		Haughton Dale Res		Haughton Dale	W 2-1
25 Oct	LC Rd2	Baxenden		Baxenden	L 4-1
8 Nov		Greenheys	2,000	North Road	W 3-1
15 Nov		Pendleton Olympic		North Road	W 3-1
22 Nov		Oughtrighton Park		Lymm	W 4-2
29 Nov		Heywood		North Road	W 5-1
6 Dec		Manchester Res		North Road	W 5-1
13 Dec		Dalton Hall		North Road	W 4-1
20 Dec		Levenshulme		Levenshulme	W 4-0
27 Dec		Heywood		Heywood	1-1
3 Jan		Eccles		North Road	0-0
10 Jan		Oughtrighton Park		North Road	W 3-2
17 Jan		Gorton		Pink Bank La	W 3-1
24 Jan		Stretford		North Road	W 12-0
31 Jan	MC Rd1	Eccles	400	North Road	W 3-2
7 Feb		Doncaster Rovers		Doncaster	W 2-2
14 Feb	MC Rd1 Replay	Eccles		Neutral	W 3-0
21 Feb		Gorton		North Road	W 6-0
7 Mar	MC Rd2	Manchester			W 3-0
14 Mar		Greenheys		North Road	W 3-1
21 Mar		West Manchester		North Road	W 5-4
28 Mar		Earlestown	1,000	Earlestown	L 2-0
4 Apr		Blackburn Olympic XI		North Road	L 1-0

Newton Heath 1884-85 (cont)

Date	Comp.	Opponents	Att	Venue	Res
11 Apr		Stretford		Stretford	0-0
18 Apr	MC SF	Dalton Hall	3,000	Neutral	W 4-3
25 Apr	MC F	Hurst	4,000	Neutral	L3-0

LC = Lancashire Cup
MC = Manchester Cup
Rd = round, SF = semi-final, F = final

Appendix 10: Early football rules

Cambridge Rules, circa 1856

In 1848 the first set unified football rules were drawn up at a meeting at Trinity College, Cambridge. These "Cambridge Rules" were agreed upon by representatives from Eton, Harrow, Rugby, Winchester and Shrewsbury schools, and academics H C Malden and G Salt. No copy of them survives, but the revised 1856 Cambridge Rules still exist in the library of Shrewsbury School.

1. This club shall be called the University Foot Ball Club.

2. At the commencement of the play, the ball shall be kicked off from the middle of the ground: after every goal there shall be a kick-off in the same way.

3. After a goal, the losing side shall kick; the sides changing goals, unless a previous arrangement be made to contrary.

4. The ball is out when it has passed the line of the flag-posts on either side of the ground, in which case it shall be thrown in straight.

5. The ball is behind when it has passed the goal on either side of it.

6. When the ball is behind it shall be brought forward at the place where it left the ground, not more than ten paces, and kicked off.

7. Goal is when the ball is kicked through the flag-posts and under the string.

8. When a player catches the ball directly from the foot, he may kick it as he can without running with it. In no other case may the ball be touched with the hands, except to stop it.

9. If the ball has passed a player, and has come from the direction of his own goal, he may not touch it till the other side have kicked it, unless there are more than three of the other side before him. No player is allowed to loiter between the ball and the adversaries' goal.

10. In no case is holding a player, pushing with the hands, or tripping up allowed. Any player may prevent another from getting to the ball by any means consistent with the above rules.

11. Every match shall be decided by a majority of goals.

   (Signed)
   H. Snow, J. C. Harkness; Eton.
   J. Hales, E. Smith; Rugby.
   G. Perry, F. G. Sykes; University.
   W. H. Stone, W. J. Hope-Edwardes; Harrow.
   E. L. Horner, H. M. Luckock; Shrewsbury.

Sheffield Rules, 1858

Formalised at the first annual general meeting of the Sheffield Football Club on 21 October 1858.

1. The kick off from the middle must be a place kick.

2. A fair catch is a catch from a player provided the ball has not touched the ground or has not been thrown from touch and is entitled to a free-kick.

3. Charging is fair in case of a place kick (with the exception of a kick off as soon as a player offers to kick) but he may always draw back unless he has actually touched the ball with his foot.

4. Pushing with the hands is allowed but no hacking or tripping up is fair under any circumstances whatever.

5. No player may be held or pulled over.

6. It is not lawful to take the ball off the ground (except in touch) for any purpose whatever.

7. The ball may be pushed or hit with the hand, but holding the ball except in the case of a free kick is altogether disallowed.

8. A goal must be kicked but not from touch nor by a free kick from a catch.

9. A ball in touch is dead, consequently the side that touches it down must bring it to the edge of the touch and throw it straight out from touch.

10. Each player must provide himself with a red and dark blue flannel cap, one colour to be worn by each side.

'The Simplest Game' (the Uppingham Rules), 1862

In 1862, J.C. Thring, a master at Uppingham School, created a new set of rules for what he called "The Simplest Game", also known as the "Uppingham Rules". Thring had been on the committee that devised the 1848 Cambridge Rules.

1. A GOAL is scored whenever the ball is forced through the goal and under the bar, except it be thrown by hand.

2. HANDS may be used only to stop a ball and place it on the ground before the feet.

3. KICKS must be aimed only at the ball.

4. A player may not kick the ball whilst in the air.

5. NO TRIPPING UP or HEEL KICKING is allowed.

6. Whenever the ball is kicked beyond the side flags, it must be returned by the player who kicked it, from the spot it passed the flag line, in a straight line towards the middle of the ground.

7. When a ball is kicked BEHIND the line of goal, it shall be kicked off from that line by one of the side whose goal it is.

8. No opposite player may stand within six paces of the kicker when he is kicking off.

9. A player is 'out of play' immediately he is in front of the ball and he must return behind the ball as soon as possible. If the ball be kicked by his own side past a player, he may not touch or kick it nor advance until one of the other side has first kicked it or one of his own side, having followed it up, has been able, when in front of him, to kick it.

10. NO CHARGING is allowed when a player is out of play – i.e. immediately the ball is behind him.

Cambridge University Rules, 1863

Drawn up in October 1863, shortly before the first meeting of the Football Association. Significant parts of these rules were adopted at an FA meeting at Freemasons Tavern, London on 24 November. This resulted in the departure of the FA's representative from Blackheath Football Club, and accelerated the codification of the Rugby game.

1. The length of the ground shall not be more than 150 yds. and the breadth not more than 100 yds. The ground shall be marked out by posts and two posts shall be placed on each side-line at distances of 25 yds. from each goal line.

2. The GOALS shall consist of two upright poles at a distance of 15 ft. from each other.

3. The choice of goals and kick-off shall be determined by tossing and the ball shall be kicked off from the middle of the ground.

4. In a match when half the time agreed upon has elapsed, the side shall change goals when the ball is next out of play. After such change or a goal obtained, the kick off shall be from the middle of the ground in the same direction as before. The time during which the game shall last and the numbers in each side are to be settled by the heads of the sides.

5. When a player has kicked the ball any one of the same side who is nearer to the opponent's goal line is OUT OF PLAY and may not touch the ball himself nor in any way whatsoever prevent any other player from doing so.

6. When the ball goes out of the ground by crossing the side lines, it is out of play and shall be kicked straight into the ground again from the point where it first stopped.

7. When a player has kicked the ball beyond the opponents' goal

line, whoever first touches the ball when it is on the ground with his hand, may have a FREE kick bringing the ball straight out from the goal line.

8. No player may touch the ball behind his opponents' goal line who is behind it when the ball is kicked there.

9. If the ball is touched down behind the goal line and beyond the line of the side-posts, the FREE kick shall be from the 25 yds. post.

10. When a player has a free-kick, no-one of his own side may be between him and his opponents' goal line and no one of the opposing side may stand within 10 yds. of him.

11. A free kick may be taken in any manner the player may choose.

12. A goal is obtained when the ball goes out of the ground by passing between the poles or in such a manner that it would have passed between them had they been of sufficient height.

13. The ball, when in play may be stopped by any part of the body, but it may NOT be held or hit by the hands, arms or shoulders.

14. ALL charging is fair; but holding, pushing with the hands, tripping up and shinning are forbidden.

(Signed)
Rev. R. Burn (Shrewsbury), Chairman
R.H. Blake Humfrey, W.T. Trench (Eton)
J.T. Prior, H.L. Williams (Harrow)
W.R. Collyer, M.T. Martin (Rugby)
W.P. Crawley (Marlborough)
W.S. Wright (Westminster)

Football Association Rules, 1863

In December 1863 the newly-founded Football Association published in its first set of rules in *Bell's Life*. Drawn up by Ebenezer Cobb Morley, the Football Association Laws had been approved at a meeting at Freemasons Tavern in London on 24 November. A hand-written note of the meeting stated that

> "The minutes of the meeting held 17th November were read and confirmed. Letters from Mr Steward (Captain of Football at Shrewsbury School), Lieut H C Moore, Mr Chambers and Mr J Bell. The Secretary laid before the meeting the rules which had been drawn up in pursuance of the resolutions passed at previous meetings which were as follows"

1. The maximum length of the ground shall be 200 yards, the maximum breadth shall be 100 yards, the length and breadth shall be marked off with flags; and the goal shall be defined by two upright posts, eight yards apart, without any tape or bar across them.

2. A toss for goals shall take place, and the game shall be commenced by a place kick from the centre of the ground by the side losing the toss for goals; the other side shall not approach within 10 yards of the ball until it is kicked off.

3. After a goal is won, the losing side shall be entitled to kick off, and the two sides shall change goals after each goal is won.

4. A goal shall be won when the ball passes between the goal-posts or over the space between the goal-posts (at whatever height), not being thrown, knocked on, or carried.

5. When the ball is in touch, the first player who touches it shall throw it from the point on the boundary line where it left the ground in a direction at right angles with the boundary line, and

the ball shall not be in play until it has touched the ground.

6. When a player has kicked the ball, any one of the same side who is nearer to the opponent's goal line is out of play, and may not touch the ball himself, nor in any way whatever prevent any other player from doing so, until he is in play; but no player is out of play when the ball is kicked off from behind the goal line.

7. In case the ball goes behind the goal line, if a player on the side to whom the goal belongs first touches the ball, one of his side shall be entitled to a free kick from the goal line at the point opposite the place where the ball shall be touched. If a player of the opposite side first touches the ball, one of his side shall be entitled to a free kick at the goal only from a point 15 yards outside the goal line, opposite the place where the ball is touched, the opposing side standing within their goal line until he has had his kick.

8. If a player makes a fair catch, he shall be entitled to a free kick, providing he claims it by making a mark with his heel at once; and in order to take such kick he may go back as far as he pleases, and no player on the opposite side shall advance beyond his mark until he has kicked.

9. No player shall run with the ball.

10. Neither tripping nor hacking shall be allowed, and no player shall use his hands to hold or push his adversary.

11. A player shall not be allowed to throw the ball or pass it to another with his hands.

12. No player shall be allowed to take the ball from the ground with his hands under any pretence whatever while it is in play.

13. No player shall be allowed to wear projecting nails, iron plates, or gutta-percha on the soles or heels of his boots.

Public School football codes in 1866

In 1866 the *Pall Mall Gazette* published a description of football played at public schools, where it had become the "predominant winter sport". The importance the schools placed on football varied, the *Gazette* claimed. At Eton, Westminster, Radley, Harrow and Winchester it was "adopted only for want of something better to do" in winter. At Marlborough, though, the game was allowed "an equal rank to cricket", while at Rugby "football is there the game of place".

School	Team size	Ground	Game length	Ball
Eton	8, 11 or 15	Ball kicked under line for goal	60-90mins	Small and light
Westminster	8, 11 or 15	Bounded by canvas screens and ropes, and "proportionately narrower than other grounds" goal-line "width of either extremity"		
Radley	8			
Harrow	11		60-90mins	"about the largest"
Winchester	11		occasionally only a few minutes, "or a dozen can be played in one match"	
Rugby	Normally 20 but up hundreds in "Grand" matches	Ball kicked over the bar for goal	Up to three days	"more oval than round"

Source: Pall Mall Gazette

The *Gazette* also detailed the major differences between the sets of rules. It noted that "most other rules (excluding Eton and Rugby) recognise a victory when the ball passes between the flags, at any height from the ground". At Eton the ball is kicked under a line for a goal, while at Rugby it has to go "over the bar".

Shinning (kicking a player below the knee) was permitted at Rugby, though "most other schools taboo it, as unsatisfactory and unnecessary". At Eton "hands could be used to stop the ball, keep it down to the feet or touch in a rouge", but the School did not permit a "fair catch" in contrast to Harrow, which allowed a "fair catch" of balls "driven from below the knee"

Unification of the Rules, 1877

On 26 February 1877 the Sheffield Association held its annual meeting. The *Glasgow Herald* reported that they

> "Have adopted a number of new laws with a view
> of bringing themselves into harmony with the
> Scottish (Glasgow) Association. The principal of
> these are with regard to what is commonly known
> as the 'three men rule', and that also relating to the
> throw in from touch. The object of bringing these
> new Scottish laws into force is that there may be a
> universal code for the game throughout the country.
> The scotch laws are approved by large numbers of
> players in the north of England and (though not
> quite agreeable to the London Association) by a
> good many in the south".

The offside rule had first appeared in the 1856 Cambridge Rules, though may date back to 1848. It stated that "more than three" opposition players must be between the goal and the most advanced attacking player when the ball is played to him. The 1863 Football Association Rules, although based on the Cambridge Rules, stated that any player in advance of a ball that had been kicked forward by a team-mate was offside. The rule, which prevented players from passing the ball forward to a teammate, resulted in a 1-2-7 "dribbling" formation becoming established. However, in 1867 the FA adopted a variation of the Cambridge offside rule, changing "more than three" to "at least three". This established the 2-2-5 "passing" game, also known as combination play, and led to the norm of two centre-backs.

Throw-ins were the other main source of disagreement. Both the 1858 Sheffield Rules and the 1863 FA Rules adopted a rugby-style lineout. The Sheffield Rules stated the ball must be thrown "straight out from touch", while the FA Rules were more specific, stating that the ball had to be thrown "at right angles with the boundary line" and had to touch the ground before being played. But by 1877 Sheffield had replaced throw-ins with a kick-ins, stating that a player "shall kick it in from where it went out and no player shall be allowed within six yards of the ball until kicked".

At its 1877 annual meeting, the Sheffield Association adopted the Scottish Association's throw-in rule, which stated that the ball may be throw in any direction the thrower may choose. The rule also stated that "the ball must be thrown at least six yards, and shall be in play when thrown in".

The Sheffield Association voted for the new rules "by large majorities" and two days later the Football Association held its annual meeting in London. The *Sheffield Telegraph,* referring to the FA as the "parent association" noted that it now "only needed the consent of the meeting to have one set of laws".

At the meeting, Old Harrovian Charles William Alcock, the FA's secretary since 1870, applauded the "liberal manner in which the Sheffield Association has come forward to reconcile the conflicting interests". This was followed by Sheffield formally adopting the London offside rule (which stated that a player must have at least three opponents nearer their own goal-line) and withdrawing its objection throw-ins. It now supported the following Clydesdale proposal for Rule 5:

"When a ball is in touch a player of the opposite
side to that which kicked it out shall throw it from
the point on the boundary line where it left the
ground in any direction the thrower may choose.
The ball must be thrown at least six yards, and shall
be in play when thrown in, but the player throwing
it shall not play it until it has been played by another
player."

The adoption of the new Rule 5 would have resulted in the first
unified set of rules for England and Scotland and was supported
by Alcock and Scottish Association Hon. Sec. J C Dick. A Todd
(Clydesdale), W Dick (Third Lanark Rifles), J F Hall and W
Wake also supported the rule change. However, C M Mackay
(Queens Park, Glasgow), A F Kinnaird (Old Etonians) and Lieut
Ruck (Royal Engineers) all opposed it and after "animated
discussions" between representatives of the 47 leading clubs, the
proposal was rejected.

The London Association was not willing to give up lineouts, a
position probably connected to England's upcoming match with
Scotland on 24 March. A far-reaching proposal by the Old
Harrovians that all players taking part in the FA Cup must
possess "some qualification, local or otherwise, which shall be
deemed to be sufficient by the committee of the association" was
also rejected. Although a definition of what constituted
"sufficient" qualification is not revealed in newspaper reports,
this appears to be an attack on professionalism. Only one
proposal was adopted – put forward by the Rochester Club as
described as "of little consequence" – which changed the
definition of holding from "below the elbow" to "extended from
the body".

After a vote on the officers for the following year, J H Clark
(Maidenhead), who presided at the meeting, was replaced by
Major F A Mandarin (Royal Engineers). Present day supporters
of Millwall FC may be interested to note that the FA
representative from Upton Park was called Mr Bastard. It's not
known whether he officiated at matches.

President
Major F A Mandarin (Royal Engineers)
Hon. Sec and treasurer
C W Alcock (Wanderers)
Committee
E H Rambridge (Swifts)
J H Clark (Maidenhead)
C E Farmer (Gitanos)
H J Foley (Pilgrims)
J Kenrick (Wanderers)
B G Jarrett (Cambridge University)
A F Kinnaird (Old Etonians)
C M Mackay (Queens Park, Glasgow)
Major Merriman (Royal Engineers)
C J Morice (Barnes)
R A Ogilvie (Clapham Rovers)
W S Rawson (Oxford University)
C L Rothora (Nottingham)
W Peirce Dix (Sheffield Association)
H J Ramage (Rochester)
S R Bastard (Upton Park)
M P Betts (Old Harrovians)

(The *Nottingham Guardian* lists C E Smith (Crystal Palace) instead of J Kenrick (Wanderers) and refers to the representative from Rochester as W K Ramage.)

However, pressure was now mounting on the FA to compromise. On 14 April the North Staffordshire Football Association was formed at a meeting of 15 clubs in Stoke. Crucially, the club's representatives unanimously agreed to adopt Sheffield Rules. Three days later the FA held an extraordinary meeting at Freemasons Tavern, London. At the meeting the new Rule 5, which replaced lineouts with Scottish throw-ins, was adopted by 38 votes to 10.

Association football finally had a set of unified rules.

Football Association Rules, 1883

Amended rules drawn up at the FA's National Conference in November 1882 and adopted by the Football Association on 8 January 1883. The corresponding 1863 rules are in bold.

1. The limits of the ground shall be: Maximum length, 200 yards; minimum length 100 yards; maximum breadth 100 yards, minimum breadth, 50 yards. The length and breadth shall be marked off with flags and touchline, and the goal shall be upright posts, eight yards apart, with a bar across them 8ft from the ground.

1. The maximum length of the ground shall be 200 yards, the maximum breadth shall be 100 yards, the length and breadth shall be marked off with flags; and the goal shall be defined by two upright posts, eight yards apart, without any tape or bar across them.

2. The winners of the toss shall have the option of kick-off or choice of goals. The game shall be commenced by a place kick from the centre of the ground in the direction of the opposite goal-line. The other side shall not approach within 10 yards of the ball until it is kicked off, nor shall any player on either side pass the centre of the ground in the direction of this opponents' goal until the ball is kicked off.

2. A toss for goals shall take place, and the game shall be commenced by a place kick from the centre of the ground by the side losing the toss for goals; the other side shall not approach within 10 yards of the ball until it is kicked off.

3. Ends shall only be changed at half-time. After a goal is won the losing side shall kick off, but after the change of ends at half-time the ball shall be kicked off by the opposite side from that which originally did so, and always as provided by *Law 2*.

3. After a goal is won, the losing side shall be entitled to kick off, and the two sides shall change goals after each goal is won

4. A goal shall be won when the ball has passed between the goal posts under the bar, not being thrown, knocked on, or carried by any one of the attacking side. The ball hitting the goal or boundary posts or goal bar and rebounding into play is considered in play.

4. A goal shall be won when the ball passes between the goal-posts or over the space between the goal-posts (at whatever height), not being thrown, knocked on, or carried.

(Major change: throw-ins)

5. When the ball is in touch, a player of the opposite side to that which kicked it out shall throw it in from the point on the boundary line where it left the ground. The thrower, facing the field of play, shall hold the ball above his head and throw it with both hands in any direction, and it shall be in play when thrown in. The player throwing it in shall not play until it has been played by another player.

5. When the ball is in touch, the first player who touches it shall throw it from the point on the boundary line where it left the ground in a direction at right angles with the boundary line, and the ball shall not be in play until it has touched the ground.

(Major change: offside rule)

6. When a player kicks the ball, *or throws it in from touch,* anyone of the same side who, at such moment of kicking or throwing is nearer to the opponents' goal-line is out of play, and may not touch the ball himself, or in any way whatever prevent any other player from doing so until the ball has been played, *unless there are at such moment of kicking or throwing at least three of his opponents nearer their own goal-line, but no player is out of play in the case of a corner kick, or when the ball is kicked from the goal-line, or when it has been played by an opponent.*

6. When a player has kicked the ball, any one of the same side who is nearer to the opponent's goal line is out of play, and may not touch the ball himself, nor in any way whatever

prevent any other player from doing so, until he is in play; but no player is out of play when the ball is kicked off from behind the goal line.

(Major change: corner kicks)
7. When the ball is kicked behind the goal-line by one of the opposite side, it shall be kicked off by any one of the players behind whose goal-line it went, within six yards of the nearest goal-post; but if kicked behind by any one of the side whose goal-line it is, a player of the opposite side shall kick it from within one yard of the nearest corner flag-post. In either case no other player shall be allowed within six yards of the ball until it is kicked off.

7. In case the ball goes behind the goal line, if a player on the side to whom the goal belongs first touches the ball, one of his side shall be entitled to a free kick from the goal line at the point opposite the place where the ball shall be touched. If a player of the opposite side first touches the ball, one of his side shall be entitled to a free kick at the goal only from a point 15 yards outside the goal line, opposite the place where the ball is touched, the opposing side standing within their goal line until he has had his kick.

(Major change: fair catch abolished)
8. No player shall carry, knock on, or handle the ball under any pretence whatever, except in the case of the goal-keeper, who shall be allowed to use his hands in defence of his goal, either by knocking on or throwing, but not carrying the ball. The goal-keeper may be changed during the game, but not more than one player shall act as goal-keeper at the same time, and no second player shall step in and act during any period in which the regular goal-keeper may have vacated his position.

8. If a player makes a fair catch, he shall be entitled to a free kick, providing he claims it by making a mark with his heel at once; and in order to take such kick he may go back as far as he pleases, and no player on the opposite side shall advance beyond his mark until he has kicked.

9. In no case shall a goal be scored from any free kick, nor shall the ball be again played by the kicker until it has been played by another player. The kick-off and corner flag-kick shall be free kicks within the meaning of this rule.

9. No player shall run with the ball.

11. A player shall not be allowed to throw the ball or pass it to another with his hands.

12. No player shall be allowed to take the ball from the ground with his hands under any pretence whatever while it is in play.

(Major change: jumping & charging from behind outlawed)

10. Neither tripping nor hacking, *nor jumping at a player*, shall be allowed, and no player shall use his hands to hold or push his adversary, *or charge him from behind*. A player with his back towards the opponents' goal cannot claim the protection of this rule, when charged from behind, provided, in the opinion of the umpires and referee, he, in that position, is wilfully impeding his opponent.

10. Neither tripping nor hacking shall be allowed, and no player shall use his hands to hold or push his adversary.

11. No player shall wear any nails, excepting such as have their heads driven in flush with the leather or iron plates, or gutta-percha on the soles or heels of his boots or shin guards. Any player discovered infringing this rule shall be prohibited from taking further part in the game.

13. No player shall be allowed to wear projecting nails, iron plates, or gutta-percha on the soles or heels of his boots.

12. In the event of any infringement of rule 5, 6, 8, 9 or 10, a free kick shall be forfeited to the opposite side, from the spot where the infringement took place.

13. In the event of an appeal from any supposed infringement of the rules, the ball shall be in play until a decision has been given.

(New Rule)
14. Each of the competing clubs shall be entitled to appoint an umpire, whose duties shall be to decide all disputed points when appealed to; and by mutual arrangement, a referee may be chosen to decide in all cases of difference between the umpires.

(New Rule)
15. The referee shall have the power to stop the game in the event of the spectators interfering with the game.

Appendix 11: The earliest FA Challenge Cup finals

Season	Winner	Score	Runners–up	Att.
1871–72	Wanderers	1–0	Royal Engineers	2,000
1872–73	Wanderers	2–0	Oxford University	3,000
1873–74	Oxford University	2–0	Royal Engineers	2,000
1874–75	Royal Engineers	1–1	Old Etonians	2,000
Replay	Royal Engineers	2–0	Old Etonians	3,000
1875–76	Wanderers	1–1	Old Etonians	3,500
Replay	Wanderers	3–0	Old Etonians	1,500
1876–77	Wanderers	2–1	Oxford University	3,000
1877–78	Wanderers	3–1	Royal Engineers	4,500
1878–79	Old Etonians	1–0	Clapham Rovers	5,000
1879–80	Clapham Rovers	1–0	Oxford University	6,000
1880–81	Old Carthusians	3–0	Old Etonians	4,000
1881–82	Old Etonians	1–0	Blackburn Rovers	6,500
1882–83	Blackburn Olympic	2–1	Old Etonians	8,000
1883–84	Blackburn Rovers	2–1	Queen's Park	4,000
1884–85	Blackburn Rovers	2–0	Queen's Park	12,500

All finals held at Kennington Oval except 1872-73, which was held at Lillie Bridge, London.

Appendix 12: Participation of Lancashire clubs in FA Cup

Entry into FA Challenge Cup by region

Season	Clubs entered	Lancashire clubs	Manchester clubs
1871-72	15	0	
1872-73	15	0	
1873-74	28	0	
1874-75	29	0	
1875-76	32	0	
1876-77	37	0	
1877-78	43	3	1
1878-79	43	3	1*
1879-80	54	4	0
1880-81	62	5	0
1881-82	71	10	0
1882-83	84	19	0
1883-84	100	26	2*
1884-85	114		1*

* Includes Hurst, from Ashton-under-Lyne

Bibliography

Walter Arnstein, "The Murphy Riots: A Victorian Dilemma," *Victorian Studies*, Vol. 19, No. 1 (Sept., 1975), pp. 51-71.

Peter Bailey, "'A Mingled Mass of Perfectly Legitimate Pleasures': The Victorian Middle-Class and the Problem of Leisure," *Victorian Studies*, Vol. 21, No. 1, (Autumn, 1977), pp. 7-28.

William J. Baker, "The Making of a Working-Class Football Culture in Victorian England" *Journal of Social History*, Vol. 13, No. 2 (Winter, 1979), pp 241-251.

Banham, Christopher, "*Boys of England* and Edwin J. Brett 1866-99", PhD Thesis, The University of Leeds, 2006.

David Bebbington, *Evangelicalism in Modern Britain: A History from the 1730s to the 1989s* (Baker, 1989).

Charbel Boujaoude, *Green & Gold: Newton Heath 1878-1902* (Empire, 2010).

David Chadwick, *Social and Educational Statistics of Manchester* (Cave and Sever, 1862).

P.F Clarke, *Lancashire and the New Liberalism* (Cambridge University Press, 2007).

Andrew Davies, *The Gangs of Manchester* (Milo Books, 2008).

Andrew Davies and Stephen Fielding, *Workers Worlds: Cultures and Communities in Manchester and Salford, 1880-1939* (Manchester University Press, 1992).

Brian Dobbs, *Edwardians at Play: 1890-1914* (Pelham, 1973).

Eric Dunning, *The Folk Origins of Modern Soccer* (C.R.S.S./Leicester University Press, Leicester, 1994)

-- --, *Notes on the Early Development of Soccer* (C.R.S.S./Leicester University Press, Leicester, 1994).

Robert H. Ellison and Carol Marie Engelhardt, "Prophecy and Anti-Popery in Victorian London: John Cumming Reconsidered" *Victorian Literature and Culture*, Vol. 31, No. 1 (2003), pp. 373-389.

Neal Garnham, "Both Praying and Playing: 'Muscular Christianity' and the YMCA in the North-East County Durham," *Journal of Social History*, Vol. 35, No. 2 (Winter, 2001), pp. 397-407.

Adrian Harvey, *Football: The First Hundred Years* (Routledge, 2005).

John C. Hawley, "Review - Glorious Battle: The Cultural Politics of Victorian Anglo-Catholicism," *Victorian Periodicals Review*, Vol. 30, No. 4, (Winter, 1997) pp. 404-406.

Richard Holt, *Sport and the British: A Modern History* (Clarendon, 1990).

Gary James, *Big Book of City* (James Ward, 2009)

-- --, *Manchester: A Football History* (James Ward, 2008)

-- --, *Manchester - The City Years* (James Ward, 2012)

-- --, *Manchester - The Greatest City* (Polar, 2002).

Fred Johnson, *Manchester City – A Souvenir History* (Holt

Publishing, 1930).

Patrick Joyce, "The Factory Politics of Lancashire in the Later Nineteenth Century" *The Historical Journal*, Vol. 18, No. 3 (Sept., 1975), pp 525-553.

J.E. King, "'We Could Eat the Police!': Popular Violence in the North Lancashire Cotton Strike of 1878" *Victorian Studies*, Vol. 28, No. 3 (Spring, 1985), pp. 439-471.

Donald Leinster-Mackay, *The Rise of the English Prep School* (Falmer Press, 1984).

Peter Lupson, *Thank God For Football* (Azure, 2006)

J A Mangan and James Walvin, *Manliness and Morality: Masculinity in Britain and America 1800-1940* (Manchester University Press, 1987).

Tony Mason, *Association Football and English Society, 1863-1915* (Branch Line, 1982)

Peter Mathias, *The First Industrial Nation* (Routledge, 2001).

Alan Metcalfe, "Organised Sport in the Mining Communities of South Northcumberland, 1800-1889", *Victorian Studies*, Vol. 25, No. 4 (Summer, 1982), pp. 469-495.

Denis Molyneaux, "The Development of Physical Recreation in the Birmingham District from 1871 to 1892", M.A Thesis, University of Birmingham, 1957.

David Newsome, *Godliness and Good Learning: Four Studies on a Victorian Ideal* (Cassell, 1961) .

Joseph O'Neill, *Crime City: Manchester's Victorian Underworld* (Milo Books, 2008).

Edward Parry, *What the Judge Saw* (Smith, Elder & Co, 1912).

Walter Ralls, "The Papal Aggression of 1850: A Study in Victorian Anti-Catholicism," *Church History*, Vol. 43, No. 2 (June 1974), pp. 242-256.

Cecil John Rhodes, *Last Will and Testament* (June 1902).

John Shelton Reed, *The Glorious Battle: The Cultural Politics of Victorian Anglo-Catholicism* (Vanderbilt U. Press, 1996).

Richard Sanders, *Beastly Fury* (Bantam Press, 2009).

Keith Sandiford, "The Victorians at Play: Problems in Historiographical Methodology," *Journal of Social History*, Vol. 15, No. 2 (Winter, 1981), pp 271-288.

Jack Simmons, *The Railways of Britain* (Routledge & Keegan Paul, 1965).

C E Sutcliffe & F Hargreaves, *History of the Lancashire Football Association* (George Toulmin, 1928).

Roger Swift, "Heros or Villains?: The Irish, Crime, and Disorder in Victorian England" *Albion*, Vol. 29, No. 3 (Autumn 1997) pp. 399-421.

Steven Tischler, *Footballers and Businessmen: The Origins of Professional Soccer in England* (Holmes & Meier, 1981).

Paul Toovey, *Birth of the Blues* (Paul Toovey, 2009).

John Tosh, *Masculinity and the Middle-Class Home in Victorian England* (Yale University Press, 1999).

W B Tracy & W T Pike, *Manchester and Salford at the Close of the 19th Century: Contemporary Biographies* (W T Pike & Co,

1899).

Wray Vamplew, *Industrialisation and Popular Sport in England in the Nineteenth Century* (C.R.S.S./Leicester University Press, 1994).

James Walvin, *The People's Game* (Mainstream, 1994).

Andrew Ward, *The Manchester City Story* (Breedon Books, 1984).

Timothy Weber, *Living in the Shadow of the Second Coming: American Premillennialism, 1875-1982* (U of Chicago Press, 1987).

Jonathan Wilson, *Inverting the Pyramid* (Orion, 2008).

David Winner, *Those Feet: A Sensual History of English Football* (Bloomsbury, 2005).

Percy Young, *A History of British Football* (Stanley Paul, 1968).

Primary Sources

Aberdeen Express
Athletic News
Backtrack Magazine
Belfast News Letter
Blackburn Standard
Derby Daily Telegraph
Exeter Flying Post
Football
Golden Penny
Gorton Reporter 1860-1900
Grantham Journal
Hampshire Advertiser
Hansard
Illustrated Police News
Leeds Intelligencer
Leeds Times
Lincolnshire Chronicle
Liverpool Daily Post
Liverpool Mercury
London Standard
Manchester Courier 1830-1900
Manchester Chronicle
Manchester Evening News
Manchester Guardian 1830-1900
Manchester Times 1830-1900
National Magazine
Nottingham Evening Post
Pall Mall Gazette
Preston Chronicle
Preston Guardian
Sheffield Daily Telegraph
Sheffield Independent
The Athlete
The Graphic
Truth

ABOUT THE AUTHOR

Andrew Keenan was born in 1966 in Greater Manchester, the son of Barbara Charnley and writer and journalist William Keenan.

His first game at Maine Road was on 28 December 1974, a dramatic match packed with historical resonance. Francis Lee scored a stunning winner for Derby that day, ran towards chairman Swales – the man who had sold him against his will – and shot him a look of defiant triumph. "Look at his face! Just look at his face!" shrieked Barry Davies on *Match of the Day* that night. Sadly all the author could see were the backs of fans' coats as the late arrival into the Kippax resulted in the eight-year-old being stuck half-way up the terracing.

But to this day he remembers the roar of the packed Maine Road crowd as City came onto the pitch – and the realisation that he would live out his life as a City fan.

Andrew graduated from Portsmouth Polytechnic in 1989 with a BA in history, an expensive drinks habit and an ability to swerve a cue ball. Afterwards he began a career in newspaper journalism which took him to the *Sunday Times*, the *Independent* and the *Daily Mirror*, where he became Deputy Editor of *Mirror Money*.

33950330R00123

Printed in Poland
by Amazon Fulfillment
Poland Sp. z o.o., Wrocław